YOUNG, WIRED, AND NOT WOKE

HOW THE YOUTH OF TODAY ARE REDEFINING SUCCESS, LOVE AND SELF

AF527745

Rishabh Shah

BOLD

An imprint of
Srishti Publishers & Distributors

By the same author

This book documents Rishabh's rollercoaster journey of reaching out to some of the most powerful people in India, without any 'connections'.

Breaking through their carefully-crafted media image, the book details how he opened the door to some of India's real-life influencers, and how they actually are as people.

Read his experience as he meets and learns from luminaries like Mohan Bhagwat, Rahul Gandhi, Dr Subramaniam Swamy, Late Dr. Pranab Mukherjee, PT Usha, Late Gen Bipin Rawat, Deepak Parekh, Karan Johar, AR Rahman and Syed Akbaruddin.

Scan to know more:

Praise for the author and his previous work

'...will help us learn from the best of the best, via a brilliant young man like Rishabh, who has shown how to implement those lessons...'

–Amish Tripathi
Bestselling author, Diplomat

'A multi-faceted individual, he led I.I.M.U.N., the world's largest youth-run organization... speaks volumes of his entrepreneurial acumen and leadership capabilities... This book will serve as an inspiration for future generations...'

–Ajay Piramal
Chairman, Piramal Enterprises Limited

'Rishabh has been able to respectfully lay bare the pluses and frailties of some of India's modern greats. In his original self-deprecating but insightful commentary, this is a compelling read for both young and old...'

–Boman Irani
Actor

'The way he weaves lessons of leadership and management into a very practical understanding of succeeding in the world is testament to the clarity of his insight.'

–Dr Shashi Tharoor
Member of Parliament

Srishti Publishers & Distributors
A unit of AJR Publishing LLP
212A, Peacock Lane
Shahpur Jat, New Delhi – 110 049
editorial@srishtipublishers.com

First published by Bold,
an imprint of Srishti Publishers & Distributors in 2025

Copyright © Rishabh Shah, 2025
10 9 8 7 6 5 4 3

The views expressed in this publication are those of the author alone and should not be taken as expert instructions or commands. While all attempts have been made to verify the information provided in this publication, neither the author nor the publisher assumes any responsibility for errors, omissions, or contrary interpretation of the subject matter herein.

The author asserts the moral right to be identified as the author of this work.

All rights reserved. No part of this publication may be reproduced, stored in a retrieval system, or transmitted, in any form or by any means, electronic, mechanical, photocopying, recording or otherwise, without the prior written permission of the Publishers.

Printed and bound in India

Contents

Introduction *1*

Love, Likes, 'Let's Keep It Casual' 9

Swipe, Scroll, Spiral 23

Puff, Pills and Problematic Conversations 39

Mental Health and What It Means: Mind It 53

Artificial Intelligence, Real Anxiety 69

He, She, They, Om 83

Who's the Neta of My Narrative 99

God's Plan... or Ours? 117

Hotter Than Your Ex's DM: Planet Earth 135

Hustle, Happiness and the Holy Rupee 149

Building the Country, Not Just Unicorns 165

50 Shades of Grey 179

Afterword *192*

This book is dedicated to my mother and father, who have allowed me to experiment and form my own understanding on various issues that are spoken about in the book, even if many a time we have vastly different opinions.

I stay Young, Wired, and not Woke to date, because of them.

Introduction

If India were a person, she'd be in college by now. About 18 years old. Technically seventy-seven on paper, but demographically, socially, and culturally, we're a country still figuring itself out: A little rebellious, a little confused, mostly online, trying to be global, but haunted by questions we haven't localized yet.

Over 65% of our population is below the age of thirty-five. That's almost a billion people trying to figure out careers, identities, beliefs, relationships, and purpose, while being bombarded with twenty-second reels promising happiness, six-figure salaries, and the secret to life in three easy steps.

We've been labelled a demographic dividend*, but no one's talking about the emotional EMIs we're paying, just to figure out who we are. We're the generation with ChatGPT in our hands, and yet, endless problems in our heads.

At times, we're overwhelmed, overstimulated, or both. Somewhere in the middle of it all, I feel many of us have lost the habit of thinking deeply.

How do you pause to think when your screen never pauses?

We're drowning in narratives that come without context. We're raised on Western apps, taught from colonial syllabi, and debating imported ideologies, while living in a country where our grandparents prayed to rivers and our parents still forward WhatsApp 'Good Morning' messages with sunflowers.

You can go from a video on Palestine to a lip-sync comedy to a skincare advertisement in under thirty seconds. You can learn the latest statistics on climate change and forget them the next minute because someone posted a thirst trap captioned 'burning like the ozone'.

Information is no longer the problem. *The lack of reflection is.* That's why I wrote this book.

I don't think young India is lost, far from it. I think we're just never given the space, or the Indian lens, to think. We're adopting conversations born elsewhere, without adapting them to a country where parents decide our career before zeroing down on our name.

We post reels on mental health, but whisper about therapy like it's a nefarious drug. We tweet about climate change, but don't know that the neem tree was our OG air purifier. We cancel people online for being 'toxic', but forget to ask: Where does forgiveness fit in our feed?

Over the last fifteen years, I've worked with young people, heard their rants, cheered their wins, and occasionally explained why working hard is different from hustling.

Born in the '90s, I stand at a curious crossroads, old enough to get why your dad still prints boarding passes, young enough to know why you'd rather text than call.

Through India's International Movement to Unite Nations or IIMUN, a youth movement I started in 2011, I've interacted with students from thirty-five countries and more than 220 Indian cities. From debating UN reform in Mumbai to discussing mental health in Agra, we have impacted over five crore teenagers.

One thing is clear: whether it's Ahmedabad or Amsterdam, young people everywhere face similar problems.

But in India, we don't always get to ask the tough questions.

So, this book is born from awkward conversations, embarrassing mistakes, heartbreaks (and Arijit Singh songs), late-night debates, early-morning panic, and a growing need to understand what growing up in India in 2025 really means.

We will be talking about issues that matter to you:

Mental Health: Is it a Western import, or is this a conversation that genuinely needs to happen in India? Are we helping people heal, or glamourizing pain just enough to fit it into an aesthetic reel?

Gender Identity and Expression: Are gender identity and expression the same thing? What about the alphabet soup? Do pronouns add clarity and recognition, or do they add confusion and rebellion? Is it genital mutilation or expression of identity?

Love and Relationships: Are we dating people or just chasing dopamine hits? What truly is the meaning of love? Is it another person, or is it about loving yourself?

Climate Change: Why have governments not been able to solve it? If leaders can't solve it, what can we do? Will it even matter, or is it better to focus on our lives instead?

Politics, Power, and Netas: Who's right? Who's left? What is centre? How did we get here? Who sets the narrative? How is it done? How to avoid getting caught in the narrative war?

God and Religion: Who is god? Was he a real-life Avenger or just a man we promoted to 'GOD'? Is it all business and is there any merit to religion as we know it today?

Social Media: Are we connected or disconnecting? Is it a mirror, a mask, a maze, or all at once? Are you the product or the user? Who's using whom?

Influencers: Are they reel models or role models who seem to have a solution for everything? Because if influence is the new currency, let's ask who's funding the mental bankruptcy?

Drugs: Too many teens know what it feels like to pop, puff, or trip; but very few have anyone to talk to about why they needed to in the first place. Perhaps not every Singh needs to be a Kabir. Perhaps doing MDMA at a rave is not a rite of passage. But if you've never walked that path, have you truly understood it?

Hustling, Happiness, and the Holy Rupee: What metrics evaluate happiness? Where did money come from? What is hustling? What are we buying, and what is it really costing us?

Businesses of Tomorrow: What are the businesses of the future? What do they need to focus on? Why are we obsessed with unicorns, but unable to sustain them? Is global capital good or another form of colonization?

AI: Will it take your job without asking? What is the point of learning to code when the code will soon write itself? Will AI become smarter than humans?

Morality, Values, and Ethics: When everything's a shade of grey, who decides what's right? When nanoships have replaced relationships, and feelings are communicated not through texts, but reels, what does it truly mean to be moral?

This book isn't here to hand out quick tips, rules or solve all your problems; there are enough influencers doing that. It's not here to guilt-trip you either; we have enough uncles and aunties for that.

This is here to document what I have been feeling. It is not a scholarly treatise; just my reflection on these topics. Some may infuriate you, some you might agree with, some are conclusions, and some others are a work in progress, all intended to help you see another perspective, or at least view things differently.

Importantly, this book asks:

What if we thought about these topics through our unique lens? Does India have solutions to these problems?

If we are to make sense of global issues that impact us, what does it truly mean to see through an Indian lens? And therefore, what does it mean to be Indian?

Like most of you, I hold on to my Indian passport, yet try to understand the paradox of being Indian.

We launch rockets to the moon, but eat curd before exams.

We preach non-violence but binge-watch action movies.

We have IITs, IIMs, and jugaad that slaps.

Where internet connection drops, but gossip spreads in CAPS.

We say *Atithi devo bhava* with flair, then ghost relatives when they climb the stairs.

We doom scroll through X, then rage at the West, only to quote Rumi, 'Do what feels best'.

But here's the thing: even with all these dichotomies, there's magic in the mess.

So, what is it to be truly Indian? That is something we'll tackle at the very end. Somewhere between algorithms and ancestral wisdom lies a voice we rarely hear: *our own*.

I remember moderating a session in a packed auditorium in a tier-two city when a teenager asked, 'Rishabh, I want to become an entrepreneur, but my parents want me to get a government job. Who's right?'

The hall went silent, not because the question was uncomfortable, but because everyone *wanted to know*. That one question held India's generational conflict in a nutshell: dreams versus security, purpose versus practicality, passion versus pragmatism.

And it's not just about parents. It's also us. We want to fit in with the sushi crowd, but secretly crave rajma chawal most days. We want to go to Boston to study, but not without our childhood buddy. We protest for freedom of expression, but sometimes forget that listening is part of it.

That's the real confusion: We're caught between wanting to become something else and being who we were shaped to be. Perhaps, in all this, we've forgotten who we truly are.

Well, I don't know how much I can uncover for you, because I, too, am unwrapping the layers of narratives wrapped around me. But I do it through something we rarely have: brutally honest conversations.

We're terrified of them. So, I take it head-on. Let's challenge the status quo and talk about uncomfortable truths.

Somewhere in the middle, you may get a gentle nudge to acknowledge that we all have much to discover. And that we don't need to fake it to make it. Because nothing works long-term as much as your authentic, true self.

So, who is this book for?

Apart from those grappling with the questions above, it's for:

- The teenager scrolling for meaning between memes.
- The 21-year-old who is acing her job, but forgetting how to sleep.
- The 35-year-old who wonders why success still feels like a system error.
- The parent who is trying to decode Gen Z and Alpha without

a user manual.

- The teacher who is still teaching values from textbooks printed before Tinder.
- The policymaker making a vision document for a Viksit Bharat in 2047 (though I doubt they'll read it... :P).
- And anyone who's ever paused mid-scroll to ask:

'Are we thinking our own thoughts, or just echoing the internet?'

Because if your feed is full but your mind feels foggy, it might be time to step out of the algorithm. In a world where pushing narratives is a profession, asking honest questions might just be the rebellion we need.

Let me clarify: I am no historian, politician, thought leader, guru, or social activist, though I've seen them all emerge from the non-profit I help run. That is both my greatest weakness and greatest strength; I have no ulterior motive. I have only one agenda right now: to get you to experiment.

Because in a world where everyone offers a sweet blue pill, it's time to break the matrix with a bitter red one. This book isn't a sermon. It's a conversation starter: unfiltered, curious, sarcastic when you least expect it, and deep when it matters most.

My dear mudbloods, are you ready?

Love, Likes, 'Let's Keep It Casual'

1.

Given that you are reading a book, I'll borrow what legendary lyricist Javed Akhtar Saab told me when he visited I.I.M.U.N., 'We live in a world where... Nanoships are the prologue, situationships are the introduction, and a relationship is the book.'

But you, my friends, had time for the relationship, so I'm sure you'll enjoy this chapter on love.

Let's start with a simple confession: Love is the most blissful thing you'll ever feel, and also the most confusing. It's the most written-about word in poetry, pop songs, and Pinterest quotes, yet it remains the most misunderstood. We're the generation that'll ruminate for hours after reading a Rumi quote, forgetting that sometimes it is just a line, not a life prophecy.

If someone tells you they've 'figured out' love, run! Seriously. Swipe left because love isn't a syllabus. It's not a formula. It definitely isn't something you decode through a three-minute Instagram reel by a relationship influencer who probably just got ghosted themselves.

I say this not from theory, but from experience. From broken relationships, unread messages, playing heartbreak songs on repeat, and maybe just a little too much experimentation.

I've been the over-lover. The under-communicator. The one who texted first. And the one who waited too long. So, trust me when I say: I don't know what love is. But I do know what love isn't.

You see, I grew up consuming Mills & Boon and *DDLJ*, watching Shah Rukh stretch his arms like he's offering life insurance, and now I'm living in a time of 'green flags', 'red flags', 'pink flags', and relationship advisory groups made up of friends who probably sailed (and sank) the same nanoships.

We're trying to find soulmates while juggling dating apps, aunties who judge our sexual preferences, and that one person who reacts to every story, but never texts.

Welcome to Gen Z dating where people go from 'Hey' to 'We're complicated' faster than a Hollywood film vilifies Russia.

And amidst all that chaos, love has often become… a vibe. A performance. It's less about connection and more about curation.

You're either stuck in a talking stage that never graduates, a situationship that comes with all the feels but none of the clarity, or a sneaky link that somehow becomes your emergency contact. There are soft launches, hard rejections, 'close friends only' stories, and a national ban on saying 'I like you' until the other person says it first, or until the vibe is mutually ghosted.

But here's the thing I've learnt: Not every love story needs to be forever.

Some of your most intense connections might last exactly as long as an Instagram highlight.

And that's okay.

Some 24-hour love stories will teach you more than four-year relationships ever did. Some breakups will introduce you to yourself. And some 'I miss you' texts will only remind you that you deserve better.

This chapter isn't here to judge your love story. It's here to help you reflect.

Because somewhere in the middle of all these labels and love languages, we've forgotten the most important thing: clarity.

Come, let's explore together!

1. In a world where everyone's busy manifesting their soulmate to reality, do we even need one? Or, like Krishna, can we have many? Most importantly, who is a soulmate?
2. What makes a relationship? Is it commitment? Chemistry? Or something else?
3. Benching, breadcrumbing, and situationships… do they voice the truth that didn't have labels, or are they just romantic red flags dressed up with Gen Z filters?
4. *Main ladka hoon, ladke se pyaar karta hoon*, is that wrong? What did our culture actually say about it?
5. Why are divorce rates rising in India, and what does that say about how we now view love and marriage?

I will not make the mistake of defining love. I will share my mistakes. My lessons. My not-so-proud moments. My journey, and my reflections.

Because sometimes, knowing what love isn't… helps you inch closer to what it might be for you.

And if nothing else, maybe this chapter will help you pause, question, laugh, cringe, and reflect. Love is not a trend or a quote, or even a feeling. It is a mirror.

And I hope that by the end of this, you'll see yourself a little more clearly in it.

Before 'seen' zones and softies, before pookies with bios like 'Sapiosexual | Coffee addict | 6'1 if it matters', love felt different.

For starters, love had a number. A landline number memorized like a maths formula, recited under your breath, dialled cautiously after praying her dad wouldn't be the one to pick up.

And if he did? Instant panic. Cut the call. Reset heart rate. Repeat.

There was no dual SIM, no ghosting, no spam accounts sliding in from backup handles, and no texting back in 0.2 seconds. There was just waiting. For that one phone ring. For that 'missed call' code. For any sign that the feeling might be mutual.

Communication was an effort that made the connection more… precious.

Back then, saying 'I like you' took courage, not just confidence. There was always that one school crush whose name you scribbled in the back of your notebook. You couldn't DM them. You couldn't send an emoji.

All you had was:

- A landline;
- A best friend brave enough to pass the message;
- And the hope she wouldn't laugh about it with her group at recess.

In my case? I was an introvert. So, despite the entire school knowing I had a crush on her, I couldn't muster the courage to walk up and say it. It's funny in hindsight because she eventually went on to date other people while I just watched, heartbroken, armed with silence and a bunch of unsent feelings. The twist? A few decades later, we're now friends and occasionally laugh about how 'obvious' it was. But back then? It didn't feel funny. It felt… final.

Love looked different. Relationships felt deeper. Not because we knew better, but perhaps because we loved differently. If school was about silent heartbreaks and landline codes, college was a different story altogether. I had grown up, or at least I thought I had.

I was 16, in college, and finally confident enough to talk to girls without stuttering or mentally rehearsing ten versions of 'Hi'. I had graduated from introverted crushes to actual conversations. And eventually, dating.

I met a girl in class, and like any teenager with a rom-com setting hardwired into their nervous system, I thought this was it. Infatuation grew into liking. Liking into late-night chats. Late-night chats into long walks, inside jokes, and the belief that this wasn't just romance, it was destiny. I was the forever-*wala* type. The kind who believed that if I'm dating you, I'm also subconsciously preparing a wedding guest list. (I still am, in a slightly different context, though.)

So, when disagreements began creeping in, big ones, not just where to eat, I thought love would still win. That intensity could solve the incompatibility. Spoiler alert: it didn't. It still doesn't.

When the relationship began falling apart, I couldn't digest it. I kept saying, 'This can't be the end. We're meant to be.' I broke down. Literally. Called friends. Cried. I had a full-blown meltdown.

Our families knew. They tried to intervene as if it were a national alliance falling through.

At one point, I remember her dad saying, 'She's so young. Why the pressure to commit? Let her explore. Let her live.'

I didn't get it then. Honestly, I still don't fully agree. But as I reflect:

Love isn't just about holding on.

Sometimes, it's about knowing when to let go, with dignity.

(Trust me, that breakup didn't happen with dignity!)

But no matter how intense it feels, not everything that burns bright is meant to last forever.

And not every breakup is a failure. Sometimes, it's a redirection.

Looking back, I smile. I don't know whether she does… :P Because what seemed like a personal apocalypse was actually life nudging me to grow up.

It taught me something no novel or movie ever told me. That love needs passion, yes. But it also needs a pause. It needs reflection. And it definitely needs two people growing in the same direction. Not just holding hands while walking opposite ways. Back then, we thought love was forever. Not because we had all the answers, but maybe because we didn't have so many options, filters, or self-help threads telling us what to walk away from every time someone replied with 'K'. We just… stayed. Tried. And stayed a little more.

My parents have disagreements. My grandparents had a few, too. But they didn't see a rough patch as a red flag. They didn't interpret silence as sabotage. They stuck around, sometimes out of love, sometimes out of duty, sometimes because '*log kya kahenge?*' had more influence than therapy.

Today, it's different. And I'm not saying better or worse, just… different.

We talk about boundaries more. We leave quicker. And often, we're told that the healthiest thing we can do is to 'cut off what doesn't serve your peace'. Which, in some cases, absolutely makes sense. But I wonder, are we leaving too soon sometimes? Are we too quick to call it toxic when it's just uncomfortable?

There's data that tells its own story. India had one of the lowest divorce rates in the world for decades, around 1%. But urban numbers have shifted. In cities like Mumbai and Delhi, divorce filings have increased to 30-40% over the last decade. And it makes me pause.

Is it because we're evolving? Or because we've equated effort with exhaustion? Maybe we confuse compatibility with comfort. And the minute it gets hard, when someone doesn't text back on time, forgets an anniversary, or isn't 'as emotionally available' as an Instagram post suggested they should be, we hit unfollow, unmatch, or emotionally unsubscribe.

Sometimes I wonder if we've started treating love like a smartphone. The moment it lags, we start looking for an upgrade. But perhaps love was never supposed to be seamless.

Perhaps it was meant to err, freeze, prompt us to restart.

But maybe the point was never to find someone perfect, but someone worth pausing for when things felt imperfect. If there were bad marriages, or became abusive or irreparable or drifted apart, sure.

I don't know. I'm still figuring it out. But I do know this… Some of the strongest connections I've seen didn't come from perfect compatibility, but from a shared commitment to try.

In a world constantly telling us to move on, maybe there's still value in holding on when it's real, mutual, and still growing. Then there is the other extreme, where I must clarify: 'Mine' is not the same as 'Love'.

Before you think I am some evolved person...

Let's just say I've come a long way from crying in college, but there is much more than meets the eye. Specifics of this story, we will uncover some other day... :P

You see, I wasn't always this reflective about love. There was a time when I genuinely thought relationships came with ownership tags.

My girl. My person. Mine.

And I know I'm not alone.

I've seen it in friends, relatives, that one couple who break up every two weeks but won't let each other breathe. From 16 to 60, possessiveness disguises itself as love, sometimes dressed in tradition, sometimes in romantic gestures, often in fear.

Most people don't admit it. Some don't even realize it But they'll still try to control, claim, and convince themselves that possession is protection.

I remember, in my college relationship, if someone so much as looked at her with too much enthusiasm, my body would tense up like I was in a Bollywood action scene. Not physically, of course, I've always been lean, so the only thing I could punch was his ego. The response was verbal, occasionally passive-aggressive, and almost always followed by a Coldplay playlist and existential texts to her like, 'Do you even love me anymore?'

Looking back, it's funny. But also… telling. We've grown up with movies that equate obsession with romance. When a character says, '*Tum meri ho,*' the background score swells, not alarms. And so we learn that love means checking in constantly. Wanting to know everything. Every friend. Every text. Every outfit.

'It's not that I don't trust you… I just care.'

Here's the hard truth: Love isn't CCTV.

It's not about monitoring someone's every move. It's about giving them the freedom to be and the confidence that they'll choose you anyway.

In my own journey, I've said things like, 'Why didn't you tell me you were going out? Why are you always texting that guy? Do you need to post that?'

At times, ownership is still present, perhaps not in terms of relationships, but rather in other aspects, such as work. And I know better than to think that any of those lines came from confidence.

They came from fear. Insecurity. That quiet, uncomfortable voice inside whispering, 'Maybe I'm not enough.'

Here's what I've slowly, painfully learnt. The more you try to hold someone too tightly, the more likely they will slip away. Because people aren't possessions. They're like sand. You don't get to 'own' someone just because you love them. You get to grow with them if they choose to stay. Sometimes… they don't. That, too, is part of love's weird, wonderful contract.

There are no guarantees. No warranties. No user manuals.

I've seen people try to 'fix' this with more control. Check their partner's phone. Share locations. Set rules. Here's the thing, though. You can't control love with a leash. You can't demand intimacy through interrogation. You can't force someone to stay and still call it love.

Real love is choosing. Re-choosing. Without fear. Every single day.

Which brings me to where I am today. I believe in something I call detached attachment.

To love deeply, but not cling. To care immensely, but not collapse if they leave. To hold someone close, while still keeping yourself together. To say, 'I choose you', not 'I own you'.

Because if there's one thing I've come to believe, it is this. Love doesn't grow in cages. It breathes in space.

Growing up, love was painted with a very specific brush. Boy meets girl. The girl blushes. Boy chases. The girl finally says yes. Roll credits.

Occasionally, there was that one person, neighbour or classmate whose preferences didn't fit the script. We didn't talk about it much. We giggled. We gossiped. That's evolved.

Today, thankfully, we've moved toward calling things what they are. Same-gender love isn't taboo anymore. Love doesn't ask for permission from society. It just asks for the truth from the heart. And the truth is, who you love is your business. How you treat them and how you treat yourself in that process, that's what matters.

However, I grew up in a generation where teachers preferred to *skip* the reproduction chapter in biology class. They'd mumble through diagrams, go red in the face, and tell us to read it at home, as if puberty could be self-taught.

Today? We have educators teaching full-blown gender theory in fifth grade. From skipping basics to diving into binaries, spectrums, and sexual identities, we've swung from silence to saturation. Maybe the truth lies somewhere in between.

Yes, kids deserve safe spaces. Yes, they should grow up knowing it's okay to love who they love. But maybe they should also first be allowed to grow up.

Let them figure out if they prefer cheese pizza or veggie pizza first. Let them play, stumble, laugh, sulk, and only *then* start navigating hormones and heartbreak.

You grow up thinking love will fix everything. It'll be the balm. The cure. The missing piece.

If you find the right person, the puzzle will click, and everything will make sense. And from that, we start building *our* version of love. But what is this version we're even looking for?

Because, for me, love is not what it now looks like in movies like *Kabir Singh*, where anger equals affection, and slaps are just another kind of kiss, where stalking is branded persistence, where obsession is rebranded passion. Somewhere along the way, we begin to think that toxic love is true love, because it hurts more.

It's not just Bollywood. Take *Emily in Paris*, where no one has boundaries, cheating is part of the aesthetic, and love is a carousel of French clichés in designer coats, where someone flirts with their best friend's boyfriend, then gaslights herself into believing it's 'destiny'. Apparently, it's love, as long as you say it in a bakery.

Real love isn't a photoshoot. It's not flirtation without consequence. It's not charm layered over emotional chaos. It's not about collecting experiences and people like souvenirs.

Then there's *Yeh Jawaani Hai Deewani*. We all rooted for Bunny and Naina, yes, but let's also talk about Aditi. Aditi, who once loved Avi, the classic commitment-phobic man-child with rizz but no emotional accountability. She didn't chase him. She didn't wait for him to finally grow up. She grew up instead. When she got married, it wasn't to the man she pined for, but to the man who treated her with stability and respect. And that's okay.

Because real love isn't always the loudest; it isn't always the friend-zoned guy finally getting the girl. Sometimes, real love is the quiet choice. The one who shows up. The one who makes you feel safe, not just seen.

Cinema often tells us love has to be dramatic. But in real life, love isn't always Aditya Roy Kapur-level brooding.

Remember, sometimes, it's just someone who holds your hand when the music isn't playing. It's not always poetic or perfect. It may not be the forever you imagined at sixteen with matching usernames and midnight playlists. Sometimes, it's just sitting next to someone silently and not feeling the need to do much. It's letting someone go and still smiling when their name comes up. It's not about that person; it's about the person you became because of them.

We've spent so long watching love defined by drama and the grand gestures that we've forgotten the soft stuff. The quiet check-in, 'Have you eaten?', the long waits at airport terminals, the way someone listens when you don't have the words, the comfort of not having to explain yourself, and the presence that stays even when staying is hard.

Perhaps the spark isn't everything. Maybe the real stuff isn't fireworks, it's warmth. It's showing up when you're tired. It's staying even when staying is quiet.

There may not be a perfect *Rocky or Rani*; you just need

to figure out your own definition of *Prem* in what is your own *Kahaani!*

In my case, the definition of love has continued to evolve, and since we are talking about cinema, it can best be summarized as:

Pyaar dosti hai.

Not the Ibrahim Ali Khan kind. The Shah Rukh Khan kind…:P

Yes, friendship is the foundation of love. No, love need not always be romantic. It need not even be reciprocal. It's no longer limited to one person or forever. It's a feeling I try to extend, in small ways, to all those I interact with.

A word of encouragement. A moment of presence. A genuine pause in a fast-paced world.

And I will say this, I do have a bias towards the people closest to me. I care for them deeply. I try to care consciously.

I've learnt that loving someone doesn't always mean holding on. Sometimes, it means holding space. For who they are. For who they're becoming. Even if that version grows away from you.

Love is not something you own; it's something you offer. Without ego. Without an agenda. Without expiry.

This brings me to something I've often reflected on: *'Because in the end, we all came alone. And we shall go alone.'*

Read that in isolation, and it feels lonely. Existential.

True, but heavy.

Now read it with the rest of the thought:

'Because in the end, we all came alone. And we shall go alone. But what makes life bearable and beautiful is choosing the right companions along the way. And that's what makes the journey interesting. Exciting. And infinitely more lovable.'

Makes sense, maybe?

Swipe, Scroll, Spiral

2.

I am perhaps a part of the last generation that knew what boredom felt like. I didn't grow up with smartphones. I grew up with Snake on a Nokia phone. My sister and I fought over TV remotes, not Netflix passwords. I saved files on pen drives, not on Google Drive.

When someone said, 'stream', the first thought I had was about rivers, not Spotify or YouTube. I've seen the whole spectrum from Gameboys to Wii, Orkut testimonials to WhatsApp's one-view stories, from 'How do I download a ringtone?' to 'This meme just cured my breakup'.

Today's average teenager juggles two smartphones, one official account, three spam accounts, Reddit threads and Discord channels. During COVID-19, everything went full throttle. The school moved to Zoom. Exams became PDFs. Friendships became streaks. Birthdays became stories. Breakups? No closure. Just screenshots and emotional damage.

We now live in the era of digital everything, where your entire personality can be 'someone who sends reels with no context at 3 a.m.'.

Your crush doesn't call you, they like your post 14 weeks late, and expect you to take the hint.

You're not just a student or a friend or a sibling anymore. You're also a personal brand, a content curator. Without knowing it, you are a consumer because the person you talk to the most is your phone. And note, even if you don't speak, it is still listening!

But here's the real dilemma, and by dilemma, I mean the daily KBC quiz we never signed up for:

- Is the online world empowering us, or just exhausting us?
- Are dating apps giving us more choices, or creating more confusion?
- Are spam accounts protecting our privacy, or just helping us dodge responsibility?
- Are we connecting with people, or just curating ourselves for them?
- Are influencers inspiring us, or quietly selling insecurity?
- Is content creation just a career, or a billion-dollar industry quietly shaping our values and education?
- Is the algorithm showing us what we love, or deciding what we should love?
- Most importantly, is this freedom of expression, or addiction in disguise?

We call it connecting. But are we connected? Our ancestors practised *mauna*: the power of silence. We believe in 'mute story for 24 hours' and pretend it counts as spiritual restraint. They sat under trees to hear the silence within. We scroll through reels to escape the noise outside. They embraced *tapasya*: deep focus, single-pointed effort, and discipline of the senses. We tap focus mode, only to get distracted by a vibrating notification, click on one message, and somehow end up watching a compilation titled, 'Top ten moments of the Ambani Diwali celebration'.

They closed their eyes to awaken the mind. We open new tabs to numb it. They meditated to quiet the storm inside. We binge to drown it out. Same stress. Different strategy.

But just because we're online doesn't mean we're not aligned. For a moment, allow me to swipe past the surface and look at the world of social media. Threadbare.

There was a time when social media meant being social. You didn't follow people for validation. You followed them because they were your school crush or your cousin who had moved to Canada. In its early years, social media wasn't just a tool; it was a revolution.

It connected people across borders, broke silences, and even shook regimes.

During the Arab Spring, platforms like Facebook and Twitter played pivotal roles in organizing protests and disseminating information. In Egypt and Tunisia, activists used Facebook to coordinate demonstrations, while Twitter provided real-time updates that bypassed state-controlled media.

Closer to home, social media became a lifeline during natural disasters. During the 2015 Chennai floods, residents used Twitter and Facebook to offer aid, share information about submerged areas, and coordinate rescue efforts. Similarly, during the 2018 Kerala floods, volunteer groups and organizations used WhatsApp and Facebook to publicize helpline numbers and coordinate ground-level rescues for thousands.

It was raw. It was real. More than anything, it worked.

Then came self-expression. And your social feed? It became your own season of Black Mirror, only with more filters and fewer consequences. Blogs became therapy, the desi version of *Dear Zindagi*, with background music that screamed Sufism plus existential crisis.

Captions became confessionals like mini monologues from *Tamasha*, but on Instagram, and with fewer people clapping. DPs became identity; change it, and your relatives started whispering, 'Is he depressed?'

From 'Screw it, I'm moving to Goa' reels to 'Just a small-town girl with a big-city playlist' bios, everyone's life became their own Dharma production.

One minute, it's the Kusha Kapila sarcasm; the next minute, it's mimicking Alia Bhatt in *Highway* with an acoustic guitar and a quote about freedom.

Every post was a signal. Even the ones that said 'No caption needed', which obviously meant, 'Please ask me what's wrong'.

This wasn't just content. It was storytelling. Starring you. Directed by the algorithm.

While we were busy expressing ourselves, the platforms were busy studying our expressions. Every like, every scroll, every pause on a dog video was data.

And *data, as we all know, is the new oil.*

Except this oil didn't need drilling, just attention.

Somewhere in a glass office in Menlo Park, you can almost picture Zuckerberg squinting at an analytics dashboard, leaning back with an evil grin and horns like Satan, and whispering, 'Forget Harvard. This is how I make billions.'

Facebook realized it could sell our friendships. Instagram figured out it could monetize our insecurities. And Twitter... well, Twitter just sold rage by the tweet.

What began as a digital town square became a personalized surveillance bazaar; not to control you, but to predict you. Once they could predict you, they could sell to you. Once they could sell to you, they could sell…you.

Monetization entered. With it came the makeover. Social media wasn't a playground anymore. It became a marketplace. Your photos? Brand potential. Your opinions? Money-making content. Your story? An asset to pitch.

We went from, 'This helped me express myself,' to 'this video got 12K views in an hour. Should I post part 2?'

The line between authenticity and advertising began to blur. And soon, everyone online wasn't just a user. They were a brand.

Influencers became the new entrepreneurs. Content creation became a career path. Even silence had a strategy. Governments took notice and jumped in, not with regulations, but with ring lights and creator collabs.

In India, content creation is no longer just a trend; it's being positioned as a strategic industry.

- In 2024, the Government of India launched the first-ever National Creators Awards, recognizing over 100 digital influencers across categories like storytelling, tech, education, gaming, social impact, and finance. The goal? Celebrate creators who shape public narrative.
- The MyGov platform, once built for citizen feedback, now partners with top influencers to amplify government schemes, translating policies into online polls.
- From Swachh Bharat Abhiyan to Digital India, ministries hire creators to transform slogans into snackable content.
- Even global players are in sync. Meta launched its $1 billion Creator Fund globally, tagging India as a 'key growth market'. Meanwhile, YouTube's 2022 report revealed that its creator ecosystem contributed $1.1 billion to India's GDP and supported 7,50,000 full-time equivalent jobs.
- During the 2024 elections, the Election Commission partnered with influencers to encourage first-time voters, using rap videos, memes, and trending audio to simplify democracy for Gen Z.

The message is clear: Virality is no longer vanity. It's policy. It's not 'We the People' anymore. It's 'We the Platform'.

This all sounds great. But let's reflect for a second.

Are these jobs real? Are they just distractions because we are not creating employment? Are people voting because an influencer told them to vote? More than 60% of first-time voters didn't even register to vote. And a fraction of them ended up voting.

Who are they even influencing if everyone is now an influencer?

Remember when a blue tick actually meant something? I had to earn it. Apply for it. They verified my credibility. And then I got it. I remember getting so happy that I treated myself to my favourite meal as if I had aced an exam. Now? It just means your credit card worked!

Welcome to the age of the Instagram guru, where anyone with good lighting, a half-decent camera, and a Jio connection can become an 'expert'. It's not that they're always wrong; it's that they're often unqualified, unchecked, and unbothered by nuance.

Feeling sick? Forget doctors, just follow someone who binge-watched *Grey's Anatomy* and now recommends jeera water for everything, from migraines to heartbreak. So many so-called 'real doctors' are sharing advice sourced from Pinterest, not peer-reviewed journals. Things got so out of hand that the Indian government had to step in and mandate health influencers to disclose their qualifications because, apparently, people were treating their thyroid with smoothies and brushing hacks. But how many of these influencers follow these mandatory rules?

Heartbroken? Don't worry, there's an influencer with a soft filter explaining attachment styles using metaphors. Relationship *gyaan* now comes from podcasters who themselves are 'figuring out' things. Millions share them as if they are the gospel truth.

If only people asked the girls who dated these boys what the truth was, '*Cannes nahi jaate, kaan ke neeche padti.*'

Want to get rich? There's a creator who promises you can retire at 30, as long as you buy his ₹999 masterclass that comes with a PDF, a motivational quote, and no SEBI registration. The truth? Only 2% of Indian fin-influencers are SEBI-registered, but who cares as long as they're Shark Tank-approved. All of them are nearly pushing trading apps, freedom plans and fantasy finance. Think: Are you increasing their finance or yours before you subscribe to any, 'Finance with ______' channel?

Need spiritual guidance? There's a discount code for that, too. Bhakti now meets branding, and your path to moksha includes a 'buy one, get one free' offer on essential oils.

Creators wearing branded clothes sit on a pedestal and give *pravachans* quoting 'holy books' and have built massive followings delivering these talks, often interspersed with promotional collabs. The thing is, this identity that most influencers have built isn't even real.

One day, they're talking about Aghori babas, and the next day, when they're caught without filters, the only thing Aghori about them is the naked truth that they are just putting up a front to fool viewers.

Let's not forget the undisclosed ads, the silent epidemic of the influencer age.

Protein powders they've never tasted, skincare routines that change every week depending on the sponsor, all promoted without the mandatory #Ad or #PaidPartnership tags, despite clear guidelines from the Advertising Standards Council of India.

But the real twist in this tale? Even the government is playing the game. During the 2024 elections, a swarm of influencers, from fashion bloggers to food reviewers, suddenly pivoted to voter awareness, democratic responsibility, and 'why Gen Z must engage'.

Some were even podcast interviews peddling narratives for specific political parties. All great messages in theory. However, many of these were paid collaborations that were supported directly or indirectly through ministries and public platforms like MyGov.

So when your favourite creator slides from OOTD to VOTE4Bharat in one scroll, you've got to ask, 'Is this patriotism or PR in disguise.'

How many of these influencers and podcasters actually voted themselves? Because here's the thing: When a shampoo brand skips a disclosure, it's misleading.

But when a government does it, it's something else entirely.

If the same influencer who's talking about his rave culture on Saturday night is suddenly talking about national integrity by Monday…what does it say about them, and more so, those who use them?

This isn't just about influencers. It's about a system where everything, even democracy, is one step away from becoming content.

In a country where 60% of schools lack functional toilets, first the government gives them recognition and access, then realizes these influencers are just *chomus* who just want to earn money. Most of them can't even prepare adequately to put up a front.

I am sure so many of us have watched podcasts; now, go back to these podcasts and see how the person conducting the conversation cannot maintain the depth of the flow. And simply goes like hmmmm and nods their head.

But the government doesn't care; as long as you've got eyeballs, anything will work. Because in this country, nationalism also has a price tag.

Then again, let's not paint all influencers with the same brush. There is a 0.1% who are trying their bit. They use their platforms to educate, inspire, and bring about real change.

Take Revant Himatsingka, aka FoodPharmer, who exposed misleading food labels, leading to regulatory reforms in India, and who has inspired 'Sugar Boards', which map sugar levels of food items in CBSE schools. Or Abhi and Niyu, who put out patriotic content and sometimes informative videos that increase civic consciousness. That's responsible social media.

Yet, the line between virality and value has been blurred. We've equated follower counts with credibility, and likes with legitimacy. And what about the platforms themselves?

Mark Zuckerberg, once a poster boy for liberal ideals, has shifted gears.

Since 2024, Meta disbanded fact-checking initiatives, removed gender options, and realigned its algorithms, all in an effort to get a front-row seat at Donald Trump's inauguration.

While people are busy blaming the youth for being addicted to reels, maybe we should be asking, 'Who's making the reel in the first place?'

Even more so, who is running these platforms, and what are the values of those enabling these platforms? For example, if relations between India and the USA deteriorate, I will not be shocked if social media platforms are used to create pressure; their founders and companies are American, and suddenly, our creators will not have anything else to do.

The thing that is most worrisome:

Every time we get a like, our brain lights up. That's not a metaphor. That's dopamine, the same chemical released when you eat chocolate or win a bet. Only difference? Likes are cheaper, faster, and available in unlimited scrolls.

Welcome to the Validation Economy, where your confidence is built on comments, your self-worth is algorithm-approved, and the absence of a notification can ruin your day.

We've turned likes into love, comments into credibility and followers into faith. But the high fades. Always.

And then you scroll more. You compare more. You feel less.

According to a UNICEF India report (2022), 1 in 3 teenage girls reported anxiety linked directly to Instagram. In the USA, the Centres for Disease Control and Prevention reported a 60% spike in teenage depression since 2010, eerily aligned with the rise of social platforms.

In a world where everything is visible, our self-worth has become invisibly fragile. We've become addicted to being seen, but forgotten how to see ourselves. I say this not from statistics alone, but from a personal encounter that I still think about. In early 2023, I reconnected with a young girl who was once part of the I.I.M.U.N. team, someone who used to be a distant friend. She was now a full-time influencer. Verified and validated. Making serious money. Living a life that, to the outside world, looked perfect. But when we connected, she broke down. 'I trust you, Rishabh, and I trust you will understand this.'

She told me about her journey and how she always felt anxious. No matter how well she did in her life, it never felt like enough. She didn't feel seen. She felt scanned. When the validation didn't come, she questioned whether she was worth anything. I asked her if it was her parents.

'No,' she said.

Her friends?

'No.'

Relatives?

Still no. Then, what was it?

That's when I asked, 'How much time do you spend consuming content?'

She checked. Eight hours a day. She posted every day. Multiple stories. Engagement-boosting hacks. I scrolled through her profile that night, and it was flawless.

Which is precisely why it broke her. The real villain? Not a person. A platform. I suggested she take what is now called a digital detox, just for a few weeks. Step back, reset. She said, 'Rishabh, I can't. My entire family's income depends on this.'

She had no savings. Her lifestyle didn't allow for a pause. The algorithm was her manager and her master. I reminded her of her earlier self. The one who lived simply, posted occasionally, and smiled without checking angles. Back when the only filter was how much coffee to put in your mug. Eventually, a couple of weeks later, she took a break. She logged out. Breathed. Journalled. For over a month. And for the first time in months, she wasn't curating her life for strangers. Today, she's still creating, but with boundaries.

She schedules offline days. She guards her peace like it's part of her brand, because it is.

Luckily for her, it ended there, but it doesn't always end there. This same machine that gives you your daily hit of validation can easily become your nemesis. One tweet. One 15-second clip. One comment taken out of context, and boom, you're not just wrong. You're cancelled.

We no longer live in a culture of correction. We live in a culture of erasure.

Someone makes a mistake? They don't get a second chance. They get screenshots and a full-blown boycott before they can even spell 'sorry'.

Public shaming is now content. And the crowd? Always ready

with popcorn and a pitchfork.

The mob is always responsible, and they should not go overboard, but let's ask the deeper question.

Isn't the influencer equally responsible for creating a holier-than-thou image? In most cases, yes. Everyone is driven by fame, money and success.

When such rebel kids return, some give them a platform and validate them as victims.

The problem is the personality you built; it wasn't you. It was what the public wanted you to be. And you gave in. The real you became glaringly visible when you were put in your natural habitat. It is okay if you are not perfect; do not pretend to be. To such people, teach them better, and tell them to stop the act. Don't help them become victims. Otherwise, the cycle will not break.

While we're chasing likes and lighting outrage bonfires, here's why it's extremely disconcerting and reshaping our habits. It is because we have reshaped our heroes. We have gone from role models to reel models. When I was growing up, my idea of excellence wasn't viral. It was quiet. It was Rahul Dravid.

The man could walk into a stadium of 50,000 people, block out the noise, bat for six hours straight and score less than fifty runs in 300 balls, just to save a match, not to trend. He didn't post selfies. He still doesn't have a social media account. He showed up, played with dignity, and left quietly. And yet, we remembered him.

Today? You score fifty runs in thirteen balls, or the algorithm benches you. You post every day, or the feed forgets you. You keep trending, or you disappear.

We used to admire people who stood for something. Now, we follow people who just… stand out.

We celebrate quick takes over deep thoughts, volume over value, and visibility over virtue. Even our sense of beauty, depth, and worth has been hijacked.

Not by artists, but by aesthetics. Not by ideas, but by algorithms.

In another time, being authentic meant living truthfully. Now, it means having a vulnerable caption under a professionally edited reel.

What happens when we raise a generation on trending audio and attention spans that expire in 24 hours?

We get biceps filled with beer.

Talent that's become latent.

And every human in Bombay believes that you need to rebel and be blatant.

What's the solution? Let's be clear, I'm not asking you to delete Instagram. I'm not even asking you to quit social media. I'm asking you to take your power back.

If your attention is the most valuable currency in the digital world, then use your awareness mindfully. The algorithm isn't evil. It's efficient.

It feeds you more of what you react to. So if all you do is scroll rage, it'll serve you more outrage. If all you chase is aesthetics, it'll drown you in filters.

But if you choose what you follow… If you pause before you post… If you ask, 'Does this serve me, or just sedate me?' You've already hacked the system.

Here are a few simple things that help me:

- Turning off notifications;
- Following fewer people and more purpose;
- Setting a timer before opening the app;
- Replacing doom scroll with a 10-minute read or a call to a

real friend.

It's not about running away from the internet. It's about not losing yourself in it. Maybe the solution isn't in the next big app.

To the best of my knowledge, Buddha didn't say, 'Stay relevant.' He says, 'Stay present.'

We've inherited a civilizational legacy that taught *viveka* (discernment) and *vairagya* (detachment) long before Silicon Valley figured out how to hijack our dopamine loops. Maybe dharma in the digital age is just this: 'Be conscious in a world that wants you automated.'

So, no, this chapter isn't about quitting social media. It's about not letting social media quit your soul. You don't need to delete your account. Just don't delete your awareness.

Because if the world is a scroll, you should still be the one holding the screen.

Oh, and before I forget, don't forget to follow me on my only social media account on Instagram @rishabhshah2012. Haha! And do let me know how you find the book.

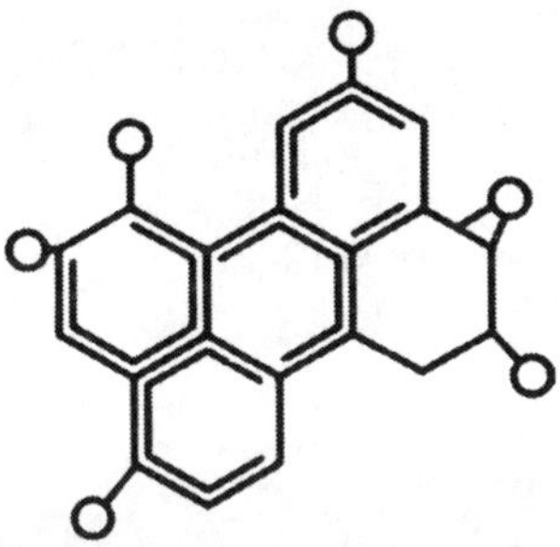

Puff, Pills and Problematic Conversations

3.

It doesn't always start with rebellion. Sometimes, it starts with boredom. Or a party where everyone's passing something around. Or a hostel room with dim lighting, three packets of Maggi, and four people trying to feel something, after yet another exam.

Substance use doesn't knock on your door wearing devil horns. It comes dressed as belonging. A friend says, 'It's just one puff.' Another laughs, 'You're such a baby, at least try!' And before you know it, you're holding a vape that smells like blueberry, but feels like pressure.

Sometimes, it's an escape. Escape from stress, from heartbreak, from pressure, from… yourself. As I have spoken to many who do these things, first as friends and then as an elder sibling, the truth is, most teenagers don't try substances because it's fun. They try them because something hurts. Unaddressed grief. Academic or parental pressure. A heartbreak they never processed. A home that doesn't feel like home. Most do it because they want to feel less.

Our culture doesn't exactly discourage it. Bollywood, for instance, has always had a flair for the dramatic high. From *Udta Punjab's* raw, chaotic depiction of addiction to *Devdas* drinking to soothe his suffering, cinema has glamorized pain as much as it has portrayed it. The melancholic sipping, the slow-motion sadness. Somehow, it becomes poetic.

Influencer culture is no different, just better lit. Aesthetic reels with 'Saturday night bangers' and clinking glasses. Self-deprecating jokes about being 'functionally high'. Even memes make addiction look… chill.

So living in a society doesn't make it easier. We live in a world where working less is romanticized, and vices are rebranded as coping mechanisms. Drinking is called 'unwinding'.

Smoking is 'me-time'. Drugs are 'just experimenting'.

And numbing becomes... normal. Therefore, I am not surprised that so many teens I know believe, 'We vape to be seen as chill, sip to forget we're stressed, and post about it to pretend we're in control.'

But are we? People often say, 'I'll quit when I want.' Can you? Can you walk away when it no longer feels cool, but starts to feel necessary? Before we get into the science and the stories, just sit with this: If you've ever reached for something, a bottle, a joint, a pill, not to celebrate but to escape... that doesn't make you weak. It makes you human.

But if we don't talk about it, we turn something human into something hidden; that's where the real danger begins.

Here's the question no one wants to ask at the party. Is this a 'bad habit'... or just a loud cry from a quiet place? This chapter isn't here to preach. It's here to hold up a mirror.

Not to tell you what's good or bad, but to make you pause, reflect, and think. Because whether it's right or wrong… That's for you to decide.

Let me tell you my personal experience. My uncle wasn't just fun, he was magnetic. The kind of man whose laughter made you forget your worries. He had a joke for every occasion, a drink for every celebration, and a spark in his eyes that made you feel like life was a party, and he was the host.

I was young, perhaps five, when he started taking us to the Hindu Gymkhana Club. There was always food, noise, friends, and this sense that adulthood was loud and alive. He'd raise his glass with that signature grin, say something witty, and the whole table would erupt.

To me, he was everything that joy looked like. And drinking? That was just part of the ritual. It was how joy was poured into a glass. But slowly, joy began to fade. His breathing grew shallow. His hands began to tremble. First came the coughing. Then, the fatigue. Then, the diagnosis of Parkinson's.

It was like watching someone dim from the inside out. The man who once danced through weddings now needed help to sit. The voice that once lit up the room could barely form complete sentences. The body that had once carried laughter now struggled to carry itself.

It's been fifteen years. He can't walk unassisted. He needs help turning in bed. Every movement takes effort. Every breath feels borrowed. That fun, the one poured into shot glasses and celebrated in smoky rooms, came at a cost.

And the bill? It didn't arrive at 30. Or 40. It arrived late, but without mercy. So, for me, alcohol and smoking have never held any appeal. Not because I think I'm better than anyone who drinks. Not because I live some ultra-monk-like life. But simply because I've seen what they can do. Up close. Quietly. Over time.

Consider someone telling you, 'A glass of wine a day is good for your heart.' That came from a decades-old study called the French Paradox, which claimed that moderate wine consumption in France led to lower rates of heart disease despite diets rich in cheese and red meat.

What didn't they tell you is this: other factors might be influencing the result, but weren't taken into account. In this case:

- The French lifestyle, more walking, smaller portions, less processed food.
- Fresh ingredients and home-cooked meals.

- Healthcare systems and stress levels.
- Cultural norms (like slower meals and stronger family/social bonds).

Maybe it wasn't the wine keeping their hearts healthy; maybe it was everything else they were doing. Newer, large-scale meta-analysis now show that even 'moderate' alcohol use increases the risk of cancer, heart failure, liver disease, and ironically, mental health issues.

Also, check who sponsors every 'alcohol is healthy' study. A foundation? But who funds the foundation? Usually, the same people who sell the product. That said, smoking and drinking are just two characters in the larger cast.

Because today, substances come in sleeker packaging. USB-sized vapes that smell like rose sorbet, pills that promise focus, syrups that help you chill, and new-age drugs dressed as mindfulness enhancers.

Let's take a look at some of the favourites:

1. Vapes

They look harmless. They smell like all things fresh, good and sweet. And they fit into your palm like a secret. But most vapes contain nicotine, a highly addictive substance that alters how your brain forms habits. Especially when you're still a teenager.

They don't just damage your lungs. They interfere with your sleep. And they can leave you feeling foggy without even knowing why.

2. Prescription Pills

ADHD meds without a prescription. Anti-anxiety tablets taken before parties. Sleeping pills are used not for rest, but to escape. They weren't meant to be casual. They're powerful when prescribed. But dangerous when used just to keep up, shut down, or zone out.

3. Lean Syrups and Mixes

Cough syrup with codeine. Mixed with soda. Sometimes topped with sugar. It's got a nickname, 'purple drank' and a whole following online. But it slows your breathing. It weakens your nervous system. And quickly builds dependency.

4. Weed

It's legal in many parts of the world, but legal doesn't mean harmless. Especially not for a teenage brain. Weed usage has been linked to:

- Poor memory;
- Lower motivation;
- Higher anxiety or paranoia;
- And sometimes, the worsening of deeper mental health struggles.

It can calm some. It can cloud others. The question isn't, 'Is it allowed?' It is, 'Is it helping me… or hiding the original me?'

5. Social Media

We've already explored this in the last chapter. But it's worth repeating: not all addictions come in bottles or joints. Some come with blue ticks and notification bells.
A vape. A pill. A joint. A screen.

They may look different, but over time, many of them tend to leave behind the same trail. You sleep a little worse. Forget things more often. Feel just a bit more anxious than usual. Start caring less. Start drifting more.

And slowly… you lose track of who you were before all this began.

It doesn't happen in one night. But it does happen, quietly, gradually, without alarms.

Not all addictions make noise. It's like the battery running out without you using your phone, but then you realize the applications are always running in the background.

And for teenagers? The effect cuts even deeper.

Because it conditions your brain. Let's talk about how it does so.

If you're a teenager reading this, your brain is beautiful.

It's curious. Fast. Wildly creative. But you need to know something most people never told you: You are under construction. Not just emotionally. Not just socially. Not just biologically, but neurologically.

The part of your brain responsible for decision-making, self-control, and long-term planning, called the prefrontal cortex, is still wiring itself together.

The Harvard Centre on the Developing Child explains that the prefrontal cortex, responsible for critical thinking, is among the last brain regions to mature. In fact, neuroscientists say, this process continues until around age twenty-five. Think of it like the CEO of your mind, except right now, the CEO has not yet been selected.

Which means:

- You feel things deeply, but can't always name them.
- You react quickly, but process slowly.
- You know better, but sometimes you still do it anyway.

That's not failure, that's wiring. Now, here's where it gets really interesting (and important):

The teenage brain learns by repetition and rewards. Whenever you do something that feels good, whether that's getting a like on a post, taking a puff, winning a game, or hearing your boyfriend laugh, your brain releases dopamine.

Dopamine is the brain's 'feel-good' chemical. But it doesn't just reward you. It teaches you. Every time you repeat something that spikes dopamine, your brain makes a note:

'Remember this. Let's do it again.' And because the adolescent brain is hypersensitive to dopamine, more so than an adult's, the highs feel higher… and the craving grows stronger.

A 2022 National Institute on Health study found that the reward centres of teenage brains are 2 to 4 times more active than those of adults when receiving dopamine hits.

This is why teenagers:

- Take more risks;
- Are more prone to addiction;
- Feel rewards more intensely;
- Struggle more with impulse control.

A 2019 study published in *The Lancet Child & Adolescent Health* showed that early exposure to substances rewires neural pathways, increasing the likelihood of future dependency.

Think of your brain like wet cement. Everything you expose it to leaves an imprint. And over time, those imprints set into patterns. If you keep chasing dopamine through vapes, pills, or mindless reels, your brain says, '*Oh, this is what I need to feel okay.*' Not because it's true. But because it's *familiar*.

When something becomes familiar, your brain stops questioning it. Here's the magic: that same wiring can be rewired.

Because the teenage brain isn't just vulnerable, it's incredibly adaptable. Neuroplasticity is your brain's ability to change itself based on experience.

You can teach it to slow down. You can teach it to sit with discomfort. You can teach it to find joy that isn't chemically engineered.

It's not about being perfect. It's about being aware of what you're training your mind to crave.

What you repeat, you become. What you chase, you eventually believe. What you consume, starts consuming you.

Pause for a moment. Ask yourself: What am I feeding my brain right now? Is it helping me become *more myself*, or just *more numb*?

If you're a parent, teacher, mentor, or sibling reading this, please understand: They're not 'rebelling'. They're rewiring. They're not 'mad' or 'moody' for no reason. They're managing dopamine floods in their brains where the brakes aren't fully built yet. They're learning how to feel without knowing how to explain it.

Before you punish the behaviour, try to understand the wiring. What they need isn't grounding. It's design. It's a conversation. It's consistency. It's someone who doesn't just *lecture* them, but someone who can *hold space* for them, even when they're glitching.

Because nobody wakes up one day and decides, *'You know what? I think I'll try and ruin my life today.'* It doesn't work like that.

Behind every puff, pill, or pour, there's usually a story. So let me tell you one.

It was 2012. He was from Delhi, loud, sharp, and fiercely opinionated. A classic Punjabi boy with swagger in his stride and dreams in his eyes. He came from a progressive, well-read family. The kind where dinner conversations ranged from Dostoevsky to Delhi elections.

We first met at I.I.M.U.N.'s Championship Conference, our annual finale. I was organizing it and he was a participant. He wasn't on stage or at the centre, not yet. Just a teenager with a spark. He was the kid with a presence, even when he wasn't trying to be seen. Back then, social media hadn't taken over our lives. The world was still filtered through real conversations, not reels.

You got to know people the old-school way, through late-night walks after conferences, heated debates in committee sessions, and high tea breaks that lasted longer than they should. And through all of that, I got to know him. At first, he was just helping out. Then, he was leading teams. He'd moved from participant to organizer almost overnight. Always first to arrive, last to leave, and somehow, still the one with the most energy in the room.

But as time passed, something began to shift. You wouldn't notice it if you didn't know what to look for. But I always had an interest in reading between the lines. The lighter that never left his pocket. The sudden bursts of emotion. The slightly dilated pupils during meetings. And then, the more obvious things, the joints, the white dust, the snort lines were visible, hidden under the charm.

When he joined our Core Council, the body that governs everything we do, I started seeing him more often. He moved to Mumbai. And with each meeting, I started seeing through him. He was brilliant, no doubt. But his brilliance came with a cloud.

One evening, after a long event, we sat down alone. He was jittery. Restless. I didn't confront him. I just asked, 'How are you, really?' He looked at me, almost amused, and said, 'Honestly? I know you don't believe in it, but it helps me think.'

'It makes me feel like myself.'

That line stuck. What do you say to someone who thinks

their own mind isn't enough unless it's altered? I didn't say much. Not that day.

Instead, I started making him travel with me. Kept him close, not to control, but to create space. We went from city to city, working on conferences, solving problems, and meeting people from all walks of life. People questioned me on my decision to let a boy who used substances lead a department that was supposed to create substance (knowledge material) for children to learn from.

But he gave me ideas in 2013 about mental health agendas and gender identity, topics that most adults were still uncomfortable talking about. He was a visionary, for sure.

And in between the work, we talked. About ideas. About happiness. About what he was really chasing. And why he thought he needed something to 'fix' a version of himself that wasn't broken to begin with.

But recovery isn't linear. It came with withdrawal symptoms, not just physical, but emotional. There were times he would lash out, times he'd disappear, times he'd show up high, eyes glassy, rage simmering just beneath the surface.

And yet, through all of it, he worked. He argued. He showed up. I saw the fight, not just with the world, but with himself. For two years, this went on. The talks. The resistance. The breakthroughs. The relapses. Until somewhere, slowly, something began to shift. It wasn't a dramatic transformation. No rock-bottom epiphany. Just a gradual softening. Fewer excuses. More questions. A kind of inward silence I hadn't seen in him before. And then one day, he said it, casually, like he was talking about the weather, 'You know… just being around someone who's confident and clean, it made me wonder if maybe I could be too.'

It wasn't about being moral. Or pure. It was about being free.

Today, he lives in the United Kingdom. He's a clinical psychologist. Working with teenagers struggling with substance use. The same kind of kid he once was. Sometimes, we still speak. Sometimes, I just hear about him from others. And every now and then, I think back to that line, 'It makes me feel like myself.'

Because here's the thing:

He didn't quit because someone scared him. Perhaps it was because someone stayed. Because someone believed in him long enough for him to start believing in himself.

Sometimes, what saves a person isn't a rehab or a rulebook. It is presence. It is patience. It is walking beside them until they can walk on their own.

Maybe you've tried something. Maybe you're curious. Maybe you're scared someone you love is slipping. Or maybe you've already slipped.

This chapter isn't asking you to be perfect. It's just asking you to be present. Because addiction doesn't always start in darkness.

Sometimes, it starts in broad daylight. At a party. In a hostel. With music in the background and a friend saying, '*It's just one puff.*'

It starts when we laugh it off. When we call it unwinding. When we post about it like it's power, but deep down, we're just trying to feel something. Or feel less.

But healing starts the same way. Quietly. Softly. With honesty. With the company. With someone reminding you:

You don't need to be numb to be enough. You don't need to be altered to be accepted. You don't need to be high to be whole.

So if you ever feel like that, reach out. Not for the substance. But for someone who'll walk with you, until you can walk on your own.

Being the anomaly doesn't mean being alone. It just means

you're the one who decided, *'I'd rather feel everything, than forget who I am.'*

Healing isn't lonely. But eventually, remember the choice has to be yours. That's why the Gita reminds us:

Uddhared ātmanātmānaṁ nātmānam avasādayet
Ātmaiva hy ātmano bandhur ātmaiva ripur ātmanaḥ

—Bhagavad Gita 6.5

Which translates as:

Lift yourself by yourself; do not degrade yourself. For the self alone is the friend of the self, and the self alone is the enemy of the self.

You are not your urges. You are not your past. You are not your pain. You are the one who can rise from it and walk forward.

If, like me, all this is too heavy, let's simplify it:

Just remember what Johnnie Walker said, 'Keep walking'.

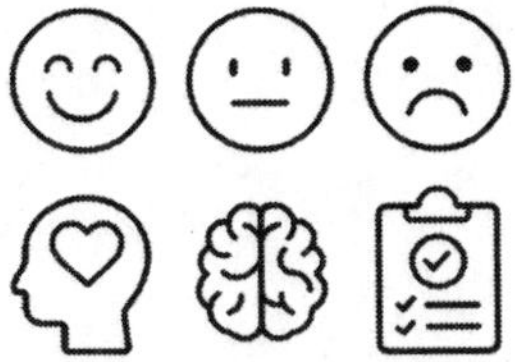

Mental Health and What It Means: Mind It

4.

If you're reading this chapter because someone told you mental health is important, that's good. They're right. If you're here because your algorithm thought you needed help, that's also fair. And if you are someone who thinks it is a 'Western concept', I've got news for you: Charaka beat Freud by about two thousand years. So, no! Mental health is not an import like pizza or Instagram. It's deeply embedded in our civilizational DNA.

Let's be real. Mental health today isn't just a concept; it's become a trend. Somewhere between self-care reels and 'I'm too depressed to do homework' memes, we've diluted the seriousness of the conversation. What began as a much-needed dialogue has often become merch, mantras, and monetized mood swings.

So, how about a different perspective? Yes, mental health is real. Yes, it matters. But no, it isn't just about disorders. It's about *well-being*; feeling grounded when the world feels wrong.

And here's the twist: What we're seeing now, especially in urban Gen Z India, is a strange mocktail of genuine emotional distress, social media mimicry, and a sprinkle of self-diagnosed drama.

Having worked with teenagers for over a decade, I've seen both ends of the spectrum.

From students who've led protests and pitched billion-dollar ideas and then completely spiral because someone left them on 'read'.

And both can happen to you. But first, let us tackle the big question: What is mental well-being?

The World Health Organization defines mental health as a state of well-being in which one realizes one's potential, copes with everyday stresses, works productively, and contributes to one's community. The Western model often treats it as the *absence* of mental illness, diagnosed via checklists and treated through therapy, medication, or both. But Indian traditions have long viewed the mind as more than a psychological organ. It's metaphysical.

According to the *Charaka Samhita*, mental health is one of the three pillars of life, along with the body and the soul. *Sattvavajaya Chikitsa* was our ancient take on psychotherapy, where healing came not just from chemical correction, but also from restoring inner harmony.

Patanjali's *Yoga Sutras* states, '*Yogaś citta-vṛtti-nirodhaḥ*. Yoga is the stilling of the fluctuations of the mind.'

In other words, good mental health isn't about being perpetually happy. It's about Clarity. Calm. Control over chaos.

Whichever model you follow, the problem is real. And it's universal. And there is evidence to show.

According to the World Health Organization, depression is now the leading cause of disability worldwide. One in seven adolescents globally lives with a mental health condition. In India, that's around four crore teenagers. That's not a phase. That's a public health emergency.

The *National Mental Health Survey* (2015-16) reported that 7.3% of Indian adolescents had a diagnosable disorder. But that was nearly a decade ago; pre-pandemic, pre-Instagram reels, and pre-the tsunami of digital overwhelm. Since then, the world and our minds have shifted.

While therapy has become almost a rite of passage in many parts of the West (like braces or gym memberships); in India, we still treat it like a scandal.

Your mum might say you're possessed. Your dad might dismiss it as a distraction.

Let me say something highly controversial, but according to me, very true.

Maybe, just maybe, that's precisely what it is.

We're distracted. By screens. By pressure. By comparison. By noise.

After all, how much clarity do we have when it comes to mundane tasks? We chant, '*Bhagwan sab theek karega*, (God will make everything alright), but we resist medication. We believe, 'Everything happens for a reason,' but shame people who seek therapy. While we must question normalizing ignorance, we must also question over-prescription, especially in teenagers.

Studies show that the usage of antidepressants in the long term can lead to dependency, emotional numbness, and difficult withdrawal. SSRIs (Selective Serotonin Reuptake Inhibitors) may work, but are not band-aids. The danger lies in treating the mind like a malfunctioning machine, not a profoundly human, complex terrain.

This isn't to vilify psychiatry. It's a reminder: medicine can manage a storm; it shouldn't become the climate.

Not every teen with sadness needs an SSRI. Sometimes, they just need sleep. Or sunlight. Or someone to ask, 'What's going on?' without judgement or diagnosis.

After all, today's youth live two lives: One online, the other, offline. And often, the pressure of the first wrecks the second.

Studies show that those who spend over three hours a day on social media have nearly double the risk of poor mental health.

Comparison is a constant. You're not just keeping up with Sharmaji's son. You're competing with 19-year-olds in Bali who have six-packs and six-figure remuneration.

And that's where your mental health takes a hit. While some influencers normalize therapy, others exploit it. There are aesthetic templates for anxiety attacks. 'Sad boi hours' isn't just a meme, it's a mindset.

Sharing helps, yes. But oversharing without reflection? Now, there's a perfect term for it.

That's just TMI, too much information. It creates noise, not healing.

In a book that urges you to reflect, it's worth asking, where did this recent phenomenon of overanalyzing ourselves even begin? Especially in the last decade?

Increased awareness? Sure. But was this increased awareness pushed by our parents?

By our schools? Not really.

Social media has become the new battlefield for mental health. And where did most of these patterns originate? You guessed it. The West.

Let's think about how this therapy trend came to be. In the West, people live independent lives; an 18-year-old is told to live by themself. They live in nuclear families at best and are taught self-dependence from a very early age. Going out for dinner alone or eating alone at a restaurant is common. While all this may have its benefits, when mental issues strike, there is no one but a therapist to talk to.

In India, the nucleus of our society is built around families. Therefore, another interesting perspective could be that your parents are your best therapists. They don't charge by the hour and don't use a rate card. Unless, of course, you are seeking therapy because of them... :P For anyone who doubts whether I believe in this concept:

At I.I.M.U.N., the non-profit I founded, we began addressing this head-on long before it was cool to do so. By 2015, we had integrated mental health as an agenda in all our conferences. Our goal is always to help students debate global issues through an Indian lens. By 2018, we had hosted 220 conferences in as many cities across India. By then, we had begun normalizing conversations about mental health even in Tier three and Tier four cities. It wasn't about making it a trend. It was a necessity.

Cut to 2025. What do we see today?

Mental health is a big business. There are apps, influencers, retreats, journals, scented candles, self-help books, and wellness podcasts peddling advice on everything from managing stress to 'healing your inner child'. There are mood trackers, breathing guides, 'emotional detox' smoothies, and content creators who begin every reel with 'Let's talk about trauma...' while holding turmeric lattes.

The mental wellness industry is growing faster than the mental health crisis itself. Somewhere between mindfulness and monetization, we need to pause.

Here's the catch: not all therapists are qualified.

In fact, what exactly have they studied, even the ones who are qualified?

Is it curing Indian patients through an Indian lens or prescribing the same Western medication?

Let me expand on the situation we have already discussed.

After all, what is considered patient-doctor confidentiality in the West can, in *some* cases, benefit from family help in the Indian context. Here, your mum and aunt know more about you than a doctor who only sees you briefly. So perhaps your doctor sharing these details may actually be beneficial.

Even in our core curriculum, we don't promote Indian texts.

So, for all the reform attempts to instil Indianness, there is a need for an Indian lens.

Another dangerous issue is how people take advice from social media influencers and WhatsApp forwards. I don't think a lot of influencers should be influencing at all (that's something you already know my views on), and WhatsApp is definitely a university no one should trust, especially on an issue this sensitive.

Yet, thanks to clever branding and filters, many have become the new high priests of healing. But let's pause for a second. Would you take financial advice from someone who's never opened a bank account? Then why take psychological advice from people who confuse validation with vulnerability? There's a rise in creators offering 'therapy-adjacent' advice like 'cut off toxic people', 'protect your energy', and 'you owe no one an explanation'. While some of it sounds empowering, blanket advice like this can lead to emotional isolation, not growth. The unspoken message becomes: if you're struggling, it must be everyone else's fault.

Spoiler alert: Real healing involves hard truths, not just viral takes. And no, it's not everyone's fault. We need to ask ourselves the million-dollar questions: Who is this propaganda serving? How much mental health awareness is a corporate branding exercise? Are we helping the youth, or just turning their struggles into profit margins?

There is now a market for everything: '5-step shadow work guides', 'affirmation decks', and whatnot. In the race to go viral with vulnerability, pain has become content. The result? Real issues get drowned in soft piano music, pastel quotes, and fake empathy. This is dangerous. For every young person genuinely in distress, there is a risk they will confuse healing with hashtags.

There's a fine line between vulnerability and victimhood,

and we're dangerously close to crossing it. These days, you'll find teenagers competing over who's more 'damaged'.

Trauma has become a status symbol. Phrases like 'I'm dead inside' or 'I have trust issues' are worn like cool badges of honour.

Online, sadness is stylized. Broken hearts get filters. Loneliness gets a Spotify playlist. Crying becomes content. Of course, sharing is valid. But healing doesn't happen just by confessing on camera. It happens through effort, therapy, perspective, and, most importantly, time.

Let's teach teens that vulnerability is brave. But healing is heroic.

Also, it starts much earlier. It begins with childhood, and with parents and schools. The first three years are critical in developing a child's understanding of adversity, resilience, and safe spaces. Parents are caught between the strict approach, where children are not allowed to do anything, and the gentle parenting approach, where children are allowed to do everything. Just like most things in life, perhaps the best approach lies somewhere in the middle.

India has over fifteen lakh schools and twenty-five crore school-going children. How many have access to a licensed school counsellor? Less than 10%. While marks, medals, and merit lists are tracked like national news, emotional well-being is barely a whisper. What should a school counsellor do? Should they focus on students' weaknesses or help them build resilience?

That is where real licensing comes in.

Take a sixteen-year-old. They're expected to choose a career, ace multiple board exams, maintain social status, act 'sanskaari', and manage heartbreak, all while navigating hormonal chaos. Most counsellors I've met call that unfair and create a victim mindset. But let's be honest: the previous generation did it too. The difference? We now have more tools and better science. But are we using them?

Let me give you my own example.

At sixteen, I was a mess of emotions. Anger was my favourite one. Hormonal imbalance was maxed out. Everyone from my grandparents to my parents told me to try yoga, prayer, and rituals. But what I really needed was a third person. A new lens. A little perspective.

I was a voracious reader, but no one pointed me toward the right books. At least no book spoke about the importance of the mind.

Then, at nineteen, when I was starting I.I.M.U.N. and exploring India's civilizational gifts, I stumbled upon meditation. If you're a teenager or a rebel like me, you probably asked the same question I did: *Why?* That's when I started reading and experimenting. I needed to know for myself, especially because we had introduced it as a one-hour session in every I.I.M.U.N. Conference.

Chant this mantra. Sit like this. Light a diya. Close your eyes. Imagine a white light. I followed it like a student prepping for boards. And for a while, it worked. My mind felt lighter, calmer, quieter. I meditated. At one point, I got my immediate team to try Vipassana, a meditation technique designed to calm the mind. But like any temporary painkiller, the calm wore off. The thought loops came back. The triggers reloaded. I was stitching the surface while the wound underneath kept reopening. Then, one day, in my mid-twenties, the right book found me.

A slender paperback by Jiddu Krishnamurti. He didn't ask me to silence the mind; he asked me to watch it. Observe the thought, don't stop it. Don't label. Don't judge. Just notice.

It sounded absurd. How do you watch your own mind? Isn't that like trying to bite your own teeth? But I tried. I sat. No chants. No visualizations. Just observation. Like a third person watching two people argue in a coffee shop, except both people were me: one reacting, the other witnessing.

Slowly, something shifted. I didn't get any less angry, but the intensity changed. I saw my thoughts arrive like trains, and realized I didn't have to board each one. Then, I discovered Ramana Maharshi. Still. Serene. Staring from black-and-white photos. His question?

'Who am I?' Not in a philosophy-class kind of way, but as a mirror, a torch.

Am I the anger I feel? The ambition I chase?

The voice in my head? Or the one watching the voice? Even though the 'I' must disappear.

And something clicked. Only intellectually, but it did.

I realized I'm not the thoughts. I'm the space they move through. The awareness behind the noise. The sky, not the clouds. Eckhart Tolle summed it best, 'You are not the mind. You are the awareness behind it.' These weren't just quotes. They were the notes on my soul. Gentle reminders. Spiritual GPS.

No, I didn't become a monk. I still lose my cool when a VIP causes a traffic jam. I still get annoyed when politicians mess up, mainly because that happens daily. But now, I notice it. I smile at it. Sometimes I even laugh at it. Because here's what I've learnt: You can't stop the waves, but you can learn to surf.

And that, to me, is real mental strength. *Not the absence of emotion, but the presence of awareness.* Does that makes sense?

Allow me to show you an Indian lens: We have always understood this mind-body connection. From the *Bhagavad Gita* to Buddhist teachings, from yoga to Ayurveda, we had entire frameworks centred on mental balance. Ayurveda talks about the *gunas,* Sattva (clarity), Rajas (restlessness), Tamas (inertia) as mental states.

But somewhere, we swapped introspection for Instagram quotes. We forgot our wisdom wasn't about renouncing the world, but rebalancing within it.

Can we go back, not to reject modern science, but to blend it with our heritage?

Daily breathwork, gratitude journalling, mindfulness, these aren't Western fads. They're Indian gifts we left unopened.

Much of this helped me through one of the most challenging phases of my life.

In 2021, I lost my grandfather. He wasn't just the head of our joint family, he was its soul. My constant. My Sunday ritual. My quiet cheerleader.

He took me on my first trip to the US. As a child, he'd take me to the Taj Mahal Hotel every Sunday, not for tea, but to buy bread from the patisserie. 'Finest bread,' he insisted. I didn't understand much, but I loved spending time with him. On the way home, we'd feed grains to pigeons.

'Be kind to animals,' he'd say. 'They don't speak, but they understand.'

He supported every hobby, cricket, chess, whatever project I'd abandon halfway. When my parents complained about my marks, he'd say, 'Let him be. Marks don't make the man. Passion does. Let him experiment till he finds it.'

So, when he passed suddenly, without warning, it felt like the axis of my world tilted. I remember it like yesterday. Our cook told me he was unwell. As I went downstairs, the water was running from the tap. And seated there was my grandad. My grandmother had broken open the bathroom door. My uncle and I carried him into the car. Just as we sat, he passed peacefully, no struggle at all. No illness. No hospital room. But no goodbye.

My parents were away. My uncle coordinated calls. I had to step up. Sorted formalities. Arranged the cremation. Welcomed relatives. And I remembered something he once said over dinner,

'Even if someone dies, don't forget to eat. Someone has to be strong for the rest.'

So I ate from Copper Chimney, his favourite. Not because I wasn't grieving, but because I knew he'd insist. I didn't cry that day. I haven't since. But I remember him every day.

Apart from my narcissistic self-portrait, a photo of him and my grandmother is the only one that sits by my bed. But do you know what disturbed me most?

People kept asking my grandmother, 'How did it happen?'

Not *how are you doing?* Not *what do you need?* Just the exact painful moment on a loop.

Why does our culture demand we relive our worst day?

'Rishabh is in a state of shock; he hasn't processed it,' they said.

Why is quiet grief seen as 'less real'?

Mental health isn't just anxiety and therapy. It's how we process pain and allow others to heal in their own way. Grief isn't always loud. Sometimes, it's silent, heavy, dignified. And it deserves space.

I don't want to leave you with takeaways, but to share my experience and let you process it as you see fit. This isn't a sermon from me to you. More, perhaps, where you are my therapist, and I am ranting... :D

Let me tell you about another kind of mental health challenge, one that didn't happen in a therapist's room, but on a stage.

It was 2023. I was invited to Delhi University's Literature Festival, a right-leaning event full of spirited students, to discuss my book *Nothing But The Truth*. Additionally, I was asked to moderate a session with the only ideologically opposite guest they had (apart from me, who they could not box): Karan Thapar.

Known for his sharp questions, he agreed to me as moderator, maybe because Google didn't show much about me. :D

I prefer to prepare in advance. But I was told: ask anything. So, I prepared generic questions.

The moment I asked something mildly challenging, he pivoted. Turned the spotlight on me.

Dismantled my question. Called me out for not reading the fine print of his book. A man twice my age. Roasting me. In front of a packed audience who loved every second.

People from the organizers, like BJP politician Swapan Das Gupta, were laughing in the first row. I still remember that sight. No one came to console me. It was humiliating. I felt small. Angry. Embarrassed. Could I observe the emotion like a Zen master? Not at all.

So, I did what worked for me. I watched a few episodes of *The Big Bang Theory*. I'm somewhere between Sheldon and Penny. :P A bit of *Sarabhai vs Sarabhai*. I distracted myself. I laughed. I broke the loop.

And I stayed. I stayed for my next session. Half the students did, too. I smiled. I spoke.

I posed for pictures. A young girl approached me and said, 'You handled it gracefully.'

That, my friends, was *my* therapy.

Because sometimes dignity is louder than defiance. Other times, it's cricket. A run. A solitary drive. As Rhonda Byrne says in *The Secret*, 'Remember that your thoughts are the primary cause of everything.'

When the mind spirals, sometimes all you need is to shift the rhythm. And when nothing works, I write. Just put it on a page. Once it's out, it doesn't seem that big anymore.

Thanks to you, neither do these episodes… :D

I don't believe everyone needs therapy. More so, not everyone can afford a thousand-rupee session. But everyone needs a way to talk to someone. Or to themselves.

Because happiness? It's a state of mind. And the mind isn't a battlefield to be won, nor a brand to build.

It's your home.

Some days, it'll be messy. Some days, it's magical. And on a few rare days, it'll feel like both. Let it. Let it breathe.

Because healing doesn't always arrive with a hashtag or a therapist's couch.

Sometimes, it comes in quiet moments. In the steam of your morning coffee, the softness of your pet's head, the voice of a friend who says, 'I've got you,' or even in a bad joke you tell yourself to keep going.

Mental health is not a destination, it's not a checkbox; it's a rhythm. A song only you can hear. Some days the music is soft, some days it's loud. Don't shame the off-notes. Don't fake the high notes. Don't exaggerate the problem in your head. Just… stay in the music.

Because if there's one thing this chapter and maybe this book wants to leave you with, it's this:

You don't need to be unshakeable.

You just need to be aware.

Of the mind. Of its tricks. And of its truths.

Keep going. Because the world doesn't need perfect minds. It needs honest ones. Awake ones. Whole ones. And definitely, most definitely, it needs yours.

Artificial Intelligence, Real Anxiety

5.

'The greatest advancements of humanity in every field will happen through and because of AI.'

But let us get one thing straight: Artificial intelligence isn't some brand-new alien species that just landed in 2025 and started helping you cheat on your history assignment.

It's been around longer than most of us have been alive. Yep, it's older than your parents' arranged marriage.

So this is how we got here:

- 1950s: Alan Turing, aka the OG computer whisperer, drops the Turing Test. Basically, he asks, 'Can machines think?'
- 1960s–80s: Computers start playing card games better than your uncle. But still, nothing out of the ordinary.
- 1997: IBM's Deep Blue beats chess champion Garry Kasparov. Boom. The first time a computer humiliates a human.
- 2002–2011: AI goes from geeky to becoming a part of your household. Automated machines start cleaning floors, Netflix starts streaming shows, and Apple's Siri becomes your pocket assistant. Suddenly, machines aren't just smart, they're *talking back*.
- 2012–2017: Enter the deep learning revolution. With algorithms inspired by the human brain (but without the mood swings), AI starts getting really good at stuff like recognizing faces, translating languages, and beating humans at games that require *strategy*, not just brute force. (Google's AlphaGo beat world champion Go player Lee Sedol in 2016, a major 'uh-oh' moment for anyone still thinking AI was just

about chess and calculators.)

- 2018–2023: AI starts doing more than answering quizzes. It writes essays, makes art, diagnoses diseases, flirts (yep), and writes Instagram captions better than you.
- Today: AI writes code, songs, ads, breakup letters, and possibly this chapter (not kidding).

But wait… What *is* AI, really?

Imagine giving your laptop a brain. Not a full human brain, more like a super-speedy intern who remembers everything and never asks for sick leave.

Technically, AI is a computer system that can do things we thought only humans could do, like learning, reasoning, problem-solving, or predicting which filter you'll use for your next story.

There are three types:

- Narrow AI: Like Siri, Alexa, or your fridge telling you you're out of milk. Good at *one* thing.
- General AI: Theoretically, a machine as smart as a human. Can do *everything* we can do, including getting confused about love.
- Superintelligent AI: Smarter than *all* humans. Think Jarvis from Iron Man meets Buddha. Capable of understanding emotion. Not here yet. But it will come soon; hopefully, it doesn't turn into Ultron.

Let's be honest. We didn't waste time. AI entered the chat, and within minutes, you had already:

- Written last-minute assignments
- Made fake Taylor Swift songs
- Generated deepfake images
- Had ChatGPT write birthday wishes

- Asked AI if your crush liked you back (Spoiler: even AI doesn't know, at least till now.)

And on the brighter side:

- Students use it to learn new languages, build apps, prep for UPSC, and pitch business ideas.
- AI is helping neurodivergent kids communicate better.
- Some are even using it to simulate therapy responses when mental health resources aren't accessible (though I don't know how much one should trust it).

So yes, AI can be a blessing or a black hole, depending on how you use it. Like most tech. Like social media. Like… pickle (amazing in moderation, unsavory if abused).

Also, remember, AI is only the sum total of everything it is fed. Therefore, the Western applications solve problems from books and lectures that are making you think in a particular direction. It may be localized to talk to you in your language, but all the data it is being given is still Western or from their lens. As the single fastest-growing online population, we also need Indian AI. But more about this some other time, for now, let's talk about a more pressing gremlin.

In group chats, in classrooms, in that awkward silence after someone says, 'Bro, ChatGPT can do your job,' these are the questions floating around:

- Will AI take over all our jobs?
- Is my degree now basically an expensive pen stand?
- Will humans become useless?
- Is there even a point to learning?
- Can AI fall in love?
- Can AI be spiritual?

- Can AI feel… shame, pride, or the sting of being left in the 'seen zone'? The anxiety isn't just technological. It's existential.

But the real thought that makes me think more isn't that *machines will become like humans*, it's that *humans will start becoming like machines*.

And so begins the rabbit hole. Shall we go deeper?

First, calculators took away our math skills. Now, AI is coming for everything, from our grammar to our grief. Once upon a time, we were told: 'Use your brain!'

Now? We're told: 'Use ChatGPT. It's faster.'

Welcome to the era where thinking is optional, where using AI, humanizing and then proofreading is the new enlightenment.

Auto-correct. Auto-summarize. Auto-translate. Auto-respond.

You don't even need to type 'Happy Birthday' anymore; your phone suggests it before you remember whose birthday it is.

Even emotions are outsourced.

Feeling sad? AI-generated playlists.

Need closure? ChatGPT can simulate a therapy session.

Got dumped? Let an AI write your 'I'm healing' Instagram caption with just the right number of heart emojis.

But the problem is that we are not just letting AI assist us. We're letting it *think* for us. And that's the real danger.

Because when intelligence becomes convenient, curiosity becomes optional.

Teachers in schools and colleges will relate to this the most. In 2023, a Stanford study found that students using AI for writing assignments scored 20–30 per cent higher. But retained 35 per cent less after a month. Translation: You passed. But you learnt… nothing.

I don't mind the use of AI; in fact, I advocate it, but A global survey revealed that 61% of Gen Z users of AI tools do not fully understand how they work. It's like driving for the first time in Mumbai but blindfolded, thinking you're bumping cars in a play zone. Well, the roads in the play zone are better than the ones we have, so... :P

Employers across industries are spotting a new trend: More polished resumes. Less original thought. Interviews are turning into a game of: *'So.. who actually wrote this CV?'*

AI might help you sound smart, act smart, and even fake smart. The real question is: Are you actually becoming smart?

According to a Microsoft survey, the average human attention span is now 8 seconds, shorter than a goldfish. Congratulations. Your brain is losing to Nemo. *And what are we losing, exactly?*

- Critical thinking: Why analyse when AI can do it?
- Originality: Why create when there's a 'generate' button?
- Reflection: Why feel when you can filter?

I am not saying AI is evil. But here's the trade-off: As AI gets smarter, are *we* getting lazier?

As it gets faster, are *we* getting shallower?

And as it becomes more 'intelligent,' are *we* becoming... replaceable? But what are you doing with the time it saves?

Are you using it to grow? Or to binge yet another conspiracy podcast about whether people think aliens exist? Don't waste your time; AI will be able to prove it soon.

Remember:

- *Efficiency without curiosity = just another algorithm;*
- *Speed without soul = just another shortcut;*
- *Knowledge without reflection = just another ChatGPT output.*

So maybe the real question isn't: Will AI make us stupid? Maybe it's: Are we letting it?

So maybe AI is making us a little lazy. A little shallow. A little too reliant. But what happens when it's not just helping you finish homework, it's applying for your job?

That's the part of the rabbit hole where things stop being cute… and start getting a little freaky. Because here's the thing: AI doesn't take lunch breaks. It doesn't get burned out. It doesn't go on mental health sabbaticals or scroll aimlessly through Instagram during work hours.

Across industries, AI is silently doing the jobs that once belonged to junior executives, customer care agents, data analysts, and that overworked guy who always wore Crocs to the office. It is the employee who never takes a break.

Well, at a closer look, some industries are already affected:

- Customer Support: That 'How can I help you today?' pop-up? Yeah, that's not Ramesh from Noida anymore. It's an AI bot from California with 99.7 per cent response accuracy and zero coffee breaks.
- Journalism: News reports, sports recaps, even obituaries; some are already written by algorithms. Imagine dying and being eulogized by a bot named Karan.
- Legal Research: AI now scans thousands of case files in seconds. Entry-level lawyers everywhere are crying softly.
- Design & Advertising: AI can now generate entire campaigns, from logos to pitch decks. Faster than your best designer can Photoshop.

So, if you know a friend who has chosen or is working in these careers, it is time perhaps to alert them. These jobs are at risk:

- Data entry;

- Coding;
- Financial analysis;
- Inventory management;
- Content generation (yep… even this). How? Well, that's a longer conversation for some other time.

But also... there are a new set of jobs to choose from:

- Prompt Engineers: People who know how to talk to AI better than me talking to a girl I like.
- AI Ethicists: The moral police of the machine world.
- Synthetic Voice Designers: Because Siri 2.0 can't sound like Siri 1.0 forever.
- Human-AI Interaction Specialists: Your job? Make robots feel less robotic. Irony, much?

Let's put it in numbers.

- Goldman Sachs: Estimated that AI will expose up to 300 million full-time jobs globally to automation, with at least 25% of the workload in these jobs being replaced by AI.
- McKinsey Global Institute: Predicted that by 2030, 14% of employees globally (375 million workers) will need to change careers due to AI advancements.
- PwC: Found that 42% of CEOs believe AI will displace more jobs than it creates, and spoke about a persistent skills gap.

And here's a brutal reality check: by 2030, it is largely believed:

- Nearly 45% of companies expect job losses due to AI.
- Only 50% expect net job growth, mainly in tech, sustainability, and education.

If people like the Godfather of AI and Nobel Prize winner in

Physics 2024, Dr Geoffrey Hinton who recently I had the privilege of interviewing at I.I.M.U.N. are to be believed... The cake is shrinking... and the recipe's changed.

But no, I don't think it's all doom and gloom. Jobs are shifting, not vanishing. Here's the catch. These new jobs require new skills. Skills that can't be downloaded. Skills that don't come with a YouTube tutorial. Skills that make you human.

Imagine this:

You slog through four years of college. Made PowerPoint presentations. Memorized facts. Passed exams. And now? The job you studied for is being done better and faster by an AI tool you didn't even know existed.

That's the new crisis. Not *'Will I get placed?'* But *'Will I stay relevant?'* And honestly? That's not just a Gen Z problem. That's a problem for everyone. We used to think blue-collar jobs were the most at risk from automation. But AI changed the narrative.

Now it's white-collar jobs, writing, coding, editing, and diagnosing that are being automated first.

Meanwhile, roles that require physical presence, creativity, emotional nuance, or just a human touch? They're safe for now. Your yoga teacher? Still employed. Your electrician and your barber? Thriving.

Your philosophy professor or therapist? Hmm… safe for a decade more, I think.

For now, AI can only mimic emotional intelligence; it can't empathize and replace you.

Our greatest power for now is handling our roommate's emotional breakdown, making a room laugh and not just sensing when something's off in your best friend's voice. But helping them by comforting them in the ways only humans can, through a hug or holding their hand.

So, should you be scared? Not really. But you *should* be aware.

Empathy is now a career skill. Creativity is now currency. Adaptability is the new job security.

So, if you're wondering what to work on next, maybe don't just learn to code. After all, now you have vibe coding, where you can use natural language prompts to generate code. It's more important to learn to connect. Learn to lead. Learn to be human.

Because that? It still can't be outsourced.

But what happens when AI can do everything? Not just our homework.

Not just our jobs. But manage our relationships.

Understand our emotions…and do *everything?*

Scenario 1:
Empathy isn't automated; it's cultivated through guided human-AI collaboration.

Elder care robots that **read subtle emotional cues**, a tremble in voice, a delay in response and know when to call a real human. Emotional literacy coaches in classrooms help children understand emotions tailored to their culture, language, and learning style. Or

Scenario 2:
Governments or platforms may use emotionally intelligent AI to **calibrate propaganda**, not just what message to show, but **when you're most vulnerable to receive it**. Teens growing up with AI friends that are always agreeable, leading to stunted emotional resilience in real-life conflicts.

Till here, it isn't that scary, but let's get nerdy for a second

Technological singularity is the hypothetical point where machines become more intelligent than us, and start improving *themselves* faster than we ever could. No humans are needed. Just code writing code, upgrades creating upgrades, bots building better bots.

Think of it like ChatGPT having a baby… and that baby is GPT-11, who's doing brain surgery while quoting Socrates and simultaneously composing a symphony. According to futurists like Ray Kurzweil, this could happen by 2045. Elon Musk thinks it'll be sooner.

Your college professor says it's nonsense. And your friend Aarav just wants to know if it means no exams.

Let's say AI reaches peak intelligence. It can code, cure diseases, make art, compose music, and maybe direct movies better than Karan Johar. Though I don't think that's happening anytime soon! Human-looking AI may even be able to procreate with humans. But then what?

If machines can do all the tasks, what's left for humans to do? This isn't just about productivity anymore. It's about purpose. Not 'What should I do for a living?'

But 'What am I living *for*?'

We've been warned not just by the Nostradamuses of the world, but by Netflix.

- In *Black Mirror*, tech reflects our worst fears, like a selfie cam that slowly steals your soul.
- In *Upload*, your consciousness can be preserved digitally, but your emotions? Still glitchy.
- In *Made in Heaven*, AI filters and surface-level perfection hide deep human dysfunction. Sounds familiar?

These weren't just bingeable sci-fi plotlines. They were flashing neon signboards saying:

If we automate everything… If we outsource every feeling… Will we still know how to be human?

Well, that's for another time. But a question I ponder over is whether machines can ever attain moksha.

Here's where our civilizational perspective leads the conversation. While the West argues about AI consciousness, India already made the distinction centuries ago:

Chaitanya, pure, unfiltered awareness. Not IQ. Not emotional intelligence. Not memory.

But the *observer is behind the mind.*

AI might have data. But does it have dharma? It might even chant mantras with perfect pronunciation, but has it ever cried?

Machines operate on instructions. Humans operate on *insight*. And no, that can't be coded. At least not till now.

For a while now, we've been fed the hustle mantra: 'Wake up. Grind. Sleep. Repeat.' We've tied our worth to output. Our identities to careers. Our self-esteem to to-do lists.

If your productivity can be automated, what's left of your *purpose*? Maybe the answer isn't in doing more. Perhaps it's in doing less, but with greater awareness.

More silence. More stillness. More slow mornings. More time spent with your thoughts, rather than outsourcing them to a voice assistant.

As a 15-year-old girl who once walked up to me and said, 'Your outfit is giving.' I replied, 'Thanks?! But giving what?'

She said, 'It's giving Rishabh.' I was still confused. Then she added, 'Your generation understands AI, but lacks AI.'

I was confused, but bro explained to me that your generation understands artificial intelligence but lacks actual intelligence. And before I could answer, she smiled and left. Was it my generation or hers? But don't worry, AI doesn't see age.

So, where does that leave us?

AI is getting faster. Smarter. More efficient. More… everything.

But here's what it's not: It's not alive. It's not conscious. It's not *you*.

For now, it still can't replicate the messy, magical mocktail of human contradiction, managing your boyfriend and yet somehow benching a guy and pocketing another. Nope, AI can't do that... :p Although I'm not sure that's the best thing to do either... :P

The algorithm is good at answering. But *you* are good at asking the right questions.

Not: 'How do I become more productive?' But, 'Why do I want to produce anything at all?'

Not: 'What can I automate?' But, 'What's worth doing even if no one sees it?'

Because your greatest power isn't in keeping up with the machine, it's in staying grounded in your meaning, your morals, your madness, your magic.

Complement what it can't be.

Let it calculate. Let it optimize. Let it filter.

You? You feel. You stumble, break, laugh, and love. You question. You forgive. You grow.

That's the human algorithm. Messy, unpredictable, but *real.*

By 2047, emotionally intelligent AI won't be about whether it can feel, but whether we still remember how to.

As the Swiss psychiatrist, Carl Jung said, 'Emotions are the chief source of becoming conscious.'

If we hand them over completely, we may become brilliant, but emotionally blind. So no, don't delete your ChatGPT account. It's just a reminder: Don't forget how to think. Don't forget how to feel. Most importantly, don't forget how to be.

You are the observer behind the mind because intelligence may be artificial.

But *you*? You're real!

He, She, They, Om

6.

When I was growing up, the world seemed binary: Boys wore blue, girls wore pink, and both awkwardly stood on opposite sides of the dance floor at school socials. Biology class gave you two options: male or female. Donald Trump, in all his loud uncertainty, seems to agree: two genders, case closed.

But is it really that simple?

As I began reading Indian scriptures and peeling through layers of our cultural history, a different picture started to form; one that wasn't black or white, but far more textured, fluid, and frankly, more fascinating.

India has always been several steps ahead of the gender conversation. While the West was still busy deciding whether the earth revolves around the sun or vice versa, Indian sages were already asking, 'Forget male and female; who am I beyond all this?'

Let's break the myth upfront: India didn't discover gender fluidity on Netflix. It was in the *Mahabharata* long before it featured in the Paris Pride Parade.

Terms like *Tritiya Prakriti* appear in ancient commentaries. Take Ardhanarishvara, half Shiva, half Parvati, embodying masculine and feminine energies as one. A being that said, 'Why choose? I'll be both.' Or Shikhandi, who started life as a woman, reborn with a vow, transformed into a man, and played a pivotal role in the Kurukshetra war. Try explaining that to a Western textbook that still thinks 'they' is only plural.

Even Arjuna, the warrior prince, spent a year identifying as Brihannala, embracing feminine expression and teaching dance, not as punishment, but as a detour. Let's not forget the *Hijra* community: not fringe, not forgotten, but once respected enough to bless weddings and advise emperors.

So, while today's world debates pronouns and bathroom laws, India's ancient lens was more transparent; gender wasn't a checkbox, but a canvas.

This chapter isn't here to cancel the West or unquestioningly glorify the East. It's to ask questions the modern world is too busy to address.

So, let's start with this: What is gender identity? What is expression? Are they the same?

Can your body say one thing and your mind another, and if so, which do you listen to?

We'll explore all of that. From myth to modernity. From Arjuna to algorithms. From he/she to Om. If you don't agree by the end, that's fine. As long as you're asking more questions than when you started, I've done my job.

Before you get tempted to say, 'Ah-ha! India was always about gender being a feeling!' And we jump to conclusions, or transitions, let's pause.

While Indian tradition certainly acknowledged exceptions, did it ever dismiss biology altogether? When I asked myself, 'What is gender identity?' I didn't go to Twitter. I went to the scriptures.

The *Bhagavad Gita* didn't hand out pronoun badges. It handed out something far more powerful; this reminder: 'You are not this body. But while you have it, know it, respect it, and act accordingly.' Is it possible we've forgotten the second half of that sentence? In much of the modern West, and via those who profess Western thought, gender identity is often described as, 'How you feel on the inside, regardless of what's on the outside.' And sure, feelings matter.

But do they override chromosomes? Can mood redefine biology?

And so, now some Western groups enlisted have seventy-two genders and counting based on internal identification.

Today, gender identity is self-declared, completely independent of your anatomy, voice, reproductive system, or even DNA.

But here's a question worth asking:

Should something so foundational, your sex, be that subjective?

Especially if you are in school or college, if you still need permission to change your school electives or for a stayover, should you be allowed to rewrite your biology?

Talking purely biologically, gender identity, or at least sex, is grounded in:

- Chromosomes (XX or XY)
- Reproductive organs (penis, vagina, uterus, testes)
- Hormones (testosterone, estrogen, etc.)
- Secondary characteristics (voice, body fat, facial hair, etc.)

These are not suggestions. They are facts. Nature, or *Prakriti*, gives you a starting point, a structure.

Do we trust it?

Or do we believe we know better?

Ancient Indian philosophy held a layered view:

- *Prakriti* (nature) defines your body; its strengths, its limitations.
- *Purusha* (consciousness) is who you are at the core; formless, genderless, eternal.
- So yes, the soul is free.

But while you're in a body, that body has its *dharma*. You don't need to become something else to evolve. Maybe you just need to understand what you already are deeply.

And what about exceptions?

Yes, our scriptures mention *Tritiya Prakriti*: People born with biological differences or who express themselves outside the binary. They were respected, not erased.

But they were seen as exceptions, not reasons to undo the foundational structure of gender altogether.

Which brings up a more complicated question: Can we honour exceptions without redefining the rule?

Maybe it's just this: You are born with a body (biological fact). You live a role aligning with that body (social and spiritual structure). And eventually, you transcend both, reaching the soul beyond form (spiritual truth).

You're allowed to feel discomfort in your body. But does discomfort mean error? Does pain mean a wrong identity, or merely growth? Could it be that the modern world is too quick to fix feelings, forgetting to listen to them?

So, what is gender identity?

Is it what you feel?

What are you biologically?

What does society expect from you?

Or what lies behind all three?

In Indian scriptures, gender identity wasn't just a feeling. It was grounded in form.

Even the exceptions acknowledged by the texts came with the caveat of biological transition or divine intervention.

Unlike today's trend of 'I am who I say I am,' Indian philosophy went deeper: 'You are not even who you were born as. You are the soul behind it all.'

But while you're here, in a body, in a society, you don't deny biology.

You live it. You transcend it. Do not overwrite it.

So yes. India recognized complexity. But it didn't cancel reality.

It didn't say gender is a feeling. It said it was a form. A function. A phase. A chance to fulfil your *dharma*.

But then came another question: Just because gender identity is biologically rooted, does that mean everyone must behave the same way?

Does a man have to roar and wrestle to be called masculine?

Must a woman wear bangles and bindis to be considered feminine?

I don't think so.

This is where civilisation showed its true sophistication: It acknowledged that you are born with a body, and therefore, a dharma. But it also gave you space to express, explore, and even blur lines in how you dress, walk, speak, or worship.

Expression was allowed to be fluid.

Today, gender expression is defined as how you show the world who you are through clothes, behaviour, voice, hair, occupation, rituals, etc.

But here's the catch: expression doesn't always align with biology. And that's okay.

The real question is: Should different expressions mean different identities?

Does wearing earrings change your chromosomes?

If a girl cuts her hair short, does that make her less feminine?

In ancient India, the answer seems to have been a calm, dignified 'No.'

The problem is that the West has confused identity and expression. India never seemed to have that confusion.

Let's look at it through the lenses of a few examples we've already discussed:

- *Brihannala* (Arjuna in exile): Arjuna spent a year disguised as a eunuch, teaching music and dance to royal women. His expression changed, but he didn't claim to no longer be a man. He adapted, not erased. That's flexibility, not fluidity.
- *Ardhanarishvara*: Shiva embodies both masculine and feminine energies. Ardhanarishvara is half male and half female, not denying gender, but representing cosmic balance. It symbolized unity, not shifting from one to another.

And a few more examples:

- Akka Mahadevi: A 12th-century female mystic who roamed without clothes, saying, 'I have given up all shame and all roles except that of a lover of the Divine.' Expression? Radically non-conforming. Identity? Fiercely rooted.
- Sufi and Bhakti saints like Meera Bai expressed devotion to Krishna by taking on the role of his lover, adopting the 'feminine' spirit of surrender regardless of their biological identity. But again, it was a devotional metaphor, not identity confusion.

But this must not detract from the fact that India not only recognized those who didn't fit male/female binaries, but respected them:

- The *Kama Sutra* mentions third-gender individuals as part of society, not as medical conditions or moral problems.
- The *Natyashastra*, India's oldest drama text, includes roles for *napumsaka* characters, giving them dignity in art.
- Hijras were seen as carrying both Shiva-Shakti energy, a bridge between worlds.

Even in modern India, where ancient traditions survive, Tamil Nadu's Koovagam festival celebrates Aravan and his transgender brides, a living tradition older than all the gender theory departments in Ivy League universities.

But, and this is crucial, the presence of Tritiya Prakriti was never used to claim gender is subjective or self-declared.

It was seen as a biological exception, a rare karmic configuration, not a daily personal choice. They were given dignity without denying the biological order.

Does making room for exceptions require erasing the structure?

Or can truth and tenderness coexist?

In my opinion, expression is art, not an identity crisis.

You could:

- Be a man and wear flowers.
- Be a woman and wield a sword.
- Be born different and still be part of a sacred rite.

I have my preferences. You will have yours.

Today, the question is: 'If I feel different, must I be different?'

Well, my two cents: *'You are already different. But your form still matters. Express with freedom. But ground yourself in truth.'*

Expression in our nation was welcomed. Exceptions were honoured. Truth was never traded for trend.

Whether you wore saffron robes, flowing sarees, or nothing at all, you are still on your way to Om. And that brings me to another polarizing part: Sex Change.

I don't think sex change is wrong, nor do I believe it is right. That is your personal decision.

What I do have are views on when and if you should start thinking about this. That, for me, is a matter of consideration.

Because I believe in design, and in understanding design before altering it. You see, we live in a time where 'how I feel' is often viewed as more real than 'how I'm built'. But is that always wise?

Should how you feel in one phase of your life, especially your teens, determine something as irreversible as your biological structure? Some might argue: isn't choice sacred? Yes, freedom matters. But 'agency' is sacred. You must be equipped with all knowledge before making a final decision.

So, let's pause and ask: Is freedom the ability to change everything at will?

Or is it a strength to understand something thoroughly before changing it?

We tell teenagers:

- You can't vote until you're eighteen.
- You can't drink until twenty-one.
- You can't sign a legal document without a guardian.

So why are we okay with letting sixteen-year-olds make decisions about hormone therapy, puberty blockers, or surgery, things that could permanently alter their bodies and mental health?

Are we giving them freedom or handing them a burden disguised as liberty?

Nature, or call it the universe, Prakriti, or just your body, has already given you a template.

Your sex, male or female, isn't an error slipped through quality control.

It results from a 13.8 billion-year evolutionary process, custom-coded through chromosomes, organs, and hormones. That isn't something you just 'change'. The universe, or nature, science, biology, karma, or god, crafted you in a special way.

You are not an accident. You are not an error in the system. You are a configuration of cosmic coding.

However, if you are an adult whose prefrontal cortex has developed, that is a different matter altogether. Your life is a consequence of your decisions.

But imagine being thirteen years old and walking into an ice cream shop. You try a new flavour.

The staff smiles and says, 'Great! That's the only flavour you'll ever be allowed to eat. Forever.'

You'd panic, right? Because at that age, you're not even sure what your favourite colour is.

So how can you be sure your current discomfort means you're in the 'wrong' body?

Is it possible the problem isn't your body but the rush to fix a feeling not fully understood yet? What's the rush?

Puberty is confusing. You're stretching, changing, and questioning. That's normal.

But today, if you express discomfort in your body, the world says, 'Ah, maybe you're trans. Let's start the process.'

That's a big leap for a small clue. While gender-change treatments are often promoted as life-saving for youth, research suggests a more complex, cautionary picture.

It's particularly concerning among adolescents whose sense of self is still developing.

As Reuters reported in a 2022 investigative review, many young people who began medical transitions as minors later expressed regret or confusion, especially when they felt rushed or inadequately assessed.

In some studies, the regret rate is as high as 75% of respondents wishing they had waited until they were older. The takeaway?

Biology isn't the villain. Rushed affirmation is.

Remember, if you are a teenager reading this: You're not broken. You're not born wrong.

You're born in a body that may feel unfamiliar, but that doesn't mean it needs to be changed. It needs to be understood.

Because maybe, just maybe, the universe didn't make a mistake.

And maybe, just maybe, this chapter wasn't written to offend you...

But there is no maybe in this: You were made purposefully.

For me, the thought of including this chapter began when an 11-year-old girl walked up to me, confident, curious, and very Gen Alpha, and asked: 'Bro, what are your pronouns?'

I smiled and said, 'First, spell pronouns.'

She did. So I answered, 'He he, ha ha.'

I laughed at my joke.

She didn't.

She turned to her friend and said, 'I thought he had rizz, but he's mid.'

And that, right there, is when I knew: Maybe we need a deeper conversation. I could be mid, and my joke most definitely could be, but that was not the point.

By now, you've probably seen it. The LinkedIn bios. The Zoom name tags. The Instagram profiles:

'Hi, I'm Kiara (she/her)'

'Hello, I'm Aarav (they/them)'

'What's up? I'm Manya (ze/zir/fluid potato).'

Don't get me wrong. If someone insists on a particular pronoun, basic courtesy says you respect it.

But let's be honest: this constant self-labelling is becoming a theatre of overcorrection.

It's one thing to be inclusive. It's another to be insecure about your existence unless it's followed by parentheses.

In the West, pronouns have somehow become proof of your morality. Get it wrong, and you're a bigot. Get it right, and you're 'doing the work'. The problem?

Language has now become activism. Every word is a landmine. Every sentence is a test.

But here's the kicker: language was supposed to serve clarity, not create confusion.

Early English pronouns were as simple as your morning chai: 'He' for a man, 'she' for a woman, and 'it' for everything else.

There was no fuss, no declarations, just words that worked perfectly until the default 'he' started speaking for everyone. Then came the feminist movements of the '60s and '70s, which looked at that 'he' monopoly and said, 'Hold up, does this reflect us all?'

Suddenly, the language had to split into 'he or she'. Eventually, 'they' emerged as a singular option, not to complicate grammar, but to ensure inclusivity.

It was a noble idea until pronouns became tangled in identity politics.

Fast forward to the early 2000s, when LGBTQ+ communities demanded language not just to describe but to define who they are.

Now, if you don't fit neatly into 'he' or 'she', you could pick pronouns like 'ze/zir' or 'xe/xem'.

What began as a bid for respect became a full-blown pronoun parade, with every email signature and social media profile daring you to list yours like an exclusive badge of honour.

By the 2010s, pronouns became less about communication and more about who could be the most politically correct. Misgender someone, and you're instantly out of touch.

In this world of verbal landmines, pronouns shifted from grammar to a chaotic identity-free-for-all, where clarity was sacrificed on the altar of inclusion.

So here we are: from 'he' and 'she' to a dizzying array of choices, the West has turned what was once a straightforward grammatical tool into an identity circus. While the intention was to create space for everyone, the end result lacked common sense.

And while it is missing sometimes in the West, let us go to the homeland of common sense: India. Sanskrit, our ancient, structured, spiritual language, handled gender 3,000 years ago. Here's how: It had three genders:

- *Pulinga* (masculine)
- *Strilinga* (feminine)
- *Napumsaka linga* (neuter/neutral)

Every noun, adjective, and verb conjugation flowed grammatically, not politically.

The sun (*surya*) is masculine.

The earth (*prithvi*) is feminine.

A tree (*vriksha*) is neuter.

Humans didn't walk around announcing their pronouns. Your identity was known, or it simply wasn't the focus. If someone was of Tritiya Prakriti, language accommodated them without a meltdown.

You didn't need to invent new pronouns; you simply respected the person, not re-engineered the sentence. In short, Sanskrit allowed gender to exist in grammar, but not dominate identity. Even today, Indian languages don't obsess over pronouns.

In Hindi, we say '*Woh aa rahe hain.* (They are coming)' whether we're talking about Ravi, Rani, or Raja Ravi Verma.

I don't think we need pronouns in bios because our tradition didn't believe in declaring identity. It is believed in discovering the self. We didn't say, 'I am he/him.' We said, 'Aham Brahmasmi': I am That. Once you say that, does it really matter what someone else calls you?

In today's India, due to the overuse of social media and pop culture references, we sometimes copy-paste Western trends without asking: 'Do we need this?'

Let's be clear:

- Respecting someone's identity? Yes.
- Declaring your pronouns to be seen as decent? No, thank you.
- Cancelling people for using the 'wrong' one by accident? Also, no.

For me, it is simple: a boy is automatically a he, and a girl automatically becomes a she.

What's the confusion? Your biology will dictate your pronouns. It's simple.

We don't need performative politics in language. We need clarity, humility, and maybe a little Sanskrit. So maybe the question isn't: 'What are your pronouns?'

Maybe it's: 'Why do you need them so badly to be seen?'

***

To all my friends who feel pronouns are the centre of the universe,

You are not your 'he' or 'she',
Nor what they expect you to be.
You are not your tag or trend,
Nor a movement you must defend.
You're not a label on a screen,

You're not your bio, bold or clean.
You are the witness, calm and wide,
The soul that watches from inside.
So wear your robe or wear your ring,
But don't forget, you're not a thing.
You're not just this or that, you see,
You are, and always were, just…
'Tat Tvam Asi.'

In this chapter, I've shared what I've understood so far: That gender identity is grounded in biology in the body you were gifted, not the mood you're in. That expression can be fluid, but identity must be rooted. That language is meant for clarity, not theatrics. That your body isn't a mistake, and changing it doesn't guarantee peace. That India knew all of this long before the West did.

This chapter isn't me pretending to be some modern-day Manu or Plato. Let me clarify that it has: 'Here's what I've read, what I've seen, what I feel, right now.'

Maybe ten years from now, I'll have read more, listened more, and evolved more.

Maybe I'll refine these views. Or maybe I'll find them truer than ever. But for now, this is my truth. You? You must discover your own.

Don't take what I've said as gospel.

Take it as a provocation, an entreaty to stop scrolling and start thinking because you don't need society's permission to be thoughtful. And you don't need social media's applause to be wise.

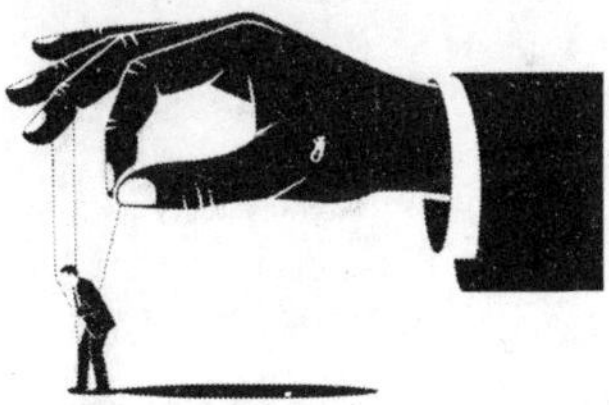

Who's the *Neta* of My Narrative

7.

Let's get one thing straight: We don't like them.

We roll our eyes when they speak, switch channels when they debate, and know at least three friends who proudly declare, 'I don't care about politics.'

But here's the twist: politics still cares. Majorly your vote, but also your life. Let me show you how they *care* about our progress at every stage of life.

Think you're too young to matter? If you're in school and worried whether your percentage is enough to get you into your dream college on open merit, who's responsible for those reservations? Politicians. If you're in your twenties, burning the midnight oil to build the next unicorn, the tax on your startup, funding laws, internet regulations, and even the 18% GST on that caramel popcorn you munch on during downtime, are all political decisions. From your thirties to fifties, wondering why house loans, petrol, or onions are pricey? Politicians again. Even if you're retired and just want your pension without bribery, guess who makes that system work or crash?

From the pothole wrecking your Activa to airport security pat-downs, or needing thirty-seven documents to prove you're Indian: It's all politics.

So yes, you might not care about them. But they care; from your cradle to your cremation.

The greater problem is: In India today, politicians don't just control *policy*. They control *perception*.

From the food you're proud of, to the movies you binge, the

reels you share, the textbooks you study, every narrative is curated, often politically.

And this isn't new.

Every five years brings a new version of the truth. We don't grow as a country. We grow confused. So, what we see isn't the full picture. It's the filtered version through the lens of power. You think you're living in a democracy. But actually, it is all hypocrisy. You're living in your bubble, and that, too, not rent-free.

Next time someone says, *'This is the India I know.'* Pause and ask, 'Who wrote that version?'

Here's the weird part.

While some of us pretend to be disinterested and say things like, 'Yaar, one vote does not matter, let's go out; it is a long weekend.' There's another species at the other end of the spectrum, the hyper-political creatures.

You've met one of these characters, I know I have!

- 'Modi is the best thing since independence,' says a friend who thinks India started in 2014 and ends at Mann Ki Baat.
- The 'everything wrong with the world started in 2014' friend who believes Modi personally melted the ice caps and purposely does not create jobs.
- And, of course, the ultra-woke intellectual activist who throws around words like fascism, genocide, and late-stage capitalism with the same ease your aunt uses 'beta'.

Before we pick teams or tune out completely, maybe it's time to pause and ask: What's the real story behind all this drama?

Let's start with the very basis on which our polity is divided: The terms left wing and right wing. They didn't even originate in India. The terms were born during the French Revolution, based on where people sat in their Parliament, on the left or the right of the King. That's it. That's the origin story.

And yet, we now use these imported labels as if they're gospel. But do these speak the truth? Well, that's for another chapter.

To those jingoists who say, 'I support the right wing because it's more Indian.' Even the term is not Indian. It's French, as French as a croissant.

Then came the Americans, who gave their own interpretations. These ideas of democracy spread across the world, but both of these are appropriated. They didn't matter in India for the longest time. It's only changed in the last 70 years. That's why, as of today, I believe:

There's nothing right in the left, and nothing left in the right.

Just like most of you, I believe all politicians are corrupt. I'd love to say no. But let's be honest, most have, at some point, dipped into the national fridge at midnight and walked away with things that did not belong to them.

When the world sleeps, India awakens to find mangoes missing from its fridge. Some stole more, some less, but all have. Some in the form of corruption, some in another way. We may not have exact data, but there is a way to find the stats for criminal activity by leaders.

Do you know that 46% of our Lok Sabha MPs have pending criminal cases? Out of whom, twenty-seven are convicted criminals! Imagine applying for a loan at your local bank and saying, 'Sir, I have four pending fraud cases and a conviction for assault.' You wouldn't even get a chair. But you can get a chair in the Parliament.

Unfortunately, everyone who cares about themselves must understand the creature called a *Neta* and its storytelling powers.

This isn't a civics lecture. I promise, no extended definitions, no textbook jargon, no diagrams with arrows pointing to Executive, Judiciary, and Legislature. This is not that book. This is your book. And in your story, politics is just one of the main characters secretly holding the pen.

Though we may need a little bit of a history check, as we go from Harappa to hashtags! To change the system, you must first understand the depth of its roots.

Politics in India didn't become flawed overnight. It evolved, just like the word charming came from 'using charms' and now has become rizz. But clearly, in politics, while there may be a lot of fizz, very few have rizz. The Indus Valley Civilisation, yes, the same one with the neatly laid-out drainage system that still puts modern Indian cities to shame, didn't leave behind campaign jingles or PR-heavy manifestos. It left behind:

- Organized cities;
- Standard weights;
- Engraved seals;
- Warehouses;
- Zero evidence of a supreme ruler.

No thrones. No coins with faces. No one claimed to have a 56-inch chest. No dictator who called for an emergency. In an era where we now crave 'strongman leaders', India started with systems over saviours. Governance wasn't about muscle; it was about the mechanism.

Then came the Mahajanapadas in the 6th century BCE. Sixteen major kingdoms and republics, not monarchies. Enter Vaishali, the OG democracy, centuries before Athens.

They had elected councils, accountable leaders and debates before making decisions. No 9 p.m. shouting matches. India never had the 'You vs. Me' Oxford-style debate. We had a Purva Paksha style of debate. In Sanskrit, *purva* means 'prior' or 'earlier,' and *paksha* means 'position' or 'side.' So purva paksha means 'the prior position,' that is, the opposing viewpoint.

It's not just acknowledging that a different opinion exists. It's deeply engaging with it, even better than your opponent might. You study their view, represent it fairly, strengthen it if needed, and then offer your rebuttal. So, you have a more nuanced understanding of the situation and don't just shout at each other. Even before we had Mauryas, Guptas, Delhi Sultans, Mughals, or the British, we understood debate, democracy, and discipline. Not universal suffrage, but the idea that you don't get to rule just because you want to. Then came the era of erosion.

- Mauryas brought efficiency, and also espionage, surveillance, and state-first control (thanks to, funnily, one of my most re-read texts, *Arthashastra*).
- Guptas (yes, the golden age of India) elevated intellect, but also turned kings into demigods.
- The Delhi Sultanate was built on power and religious supremacy, while clamping down on all religions, but Islam.
- Mughals had an administration, but no real representation. They ruled for the people, not by the people.
- Then came the British, who ironically reintroduced democracy, right after they snatched land, dignity, and sovereignty.

They gave us:

- Elections with terms and conditions;
- Bureaucracy to serve them;
- Governance, by permission slips and paperwork.

And then came 1947. Independence. Partition. A scar across maps and memories. However, a geographical boundary delineates India, that is, Bharat. It was truly only in 1950 that we gifted ourselves something remarkable: a Constitution. It declared every Indian equal, regardless of caste, gender, or bank balance. At least in theory. If that is the case, then everyone should be able to participate in politics, right?

If politics were a job, you'd need a résumé.

In India? All you need is a relative.

Every other profession has entry criteria. Want to treat patients? MBBS. Want to fly planes? Pilot's licence. Want to practice law? Law degree.

Want to govern 1.4 billion people? No degree? No experience? No clue? No problem!

You need one of the following three things:

1. A last name people recognize.
2. A wallet that could sponsor an IPL team.
3. A political godfather you're willing to applaud publicly, even when they mispronounce 'Constitution'.

Take the seventeenth Lok Sabha, for instance. Out of 7 MPs under the age of 35, 6 are dynasts. That's not youth representation; that's youth inheritance.

We don't have democracy. We have Dad-ocracy.

What about the non-dynasts who dare to try?

The hurdles include party politics that bury merit, caste equations that kill competence, and campaign costs so high that even startups look affordable.

Many from I.I.M.U.N. have tried, former participants and organizers. But hardly anyone outside of those coming from lineage have succeeded.

My suggestion: Have an entrance test and some minimum qualifications to become a politician. Let me tell you about an incident that happened closer to home. There was a girl who was a part of the team at I.I.M.U.N., and she came from a renowned political family.

She was an IB student, having finished her education in one of the most elite schools around Mumbai. She got interested in politics when she joined the organization and learnt the ropes. Today, she is a Corporator.

Call her for anything, she may not pick up, and if she picks up, if the work does not involve anything which she would benefit from, 'no, thanks' is the immediate answer. Now, this is a normal human tendency. But as a politician? Shouldn't she be helpful to all and sundry? Shouldn't the ego be kept aside?

Sadly, it is in this profession that ego is the most fragile. Corruption and ego aren't abstract; they're systematic.

The problems start with the numbers. Look at the official monthly salaries:

- Corporator: ₹20,000 – ₹35,000;
- MLA: ₹1.2 – ₹2.5 lakhs;
- MP: ₹1.5 – ₹2 lakhs;
- Union Minister: ₹2.2 – ₹2.5 lakhs;
- Prime Minister: ₹2.8 lakhs.

Compare that to:

- A mid-level software engineer: ₹1.5 lakh/month;
- A VP in a private firm:₹3–5 lakhs/month;
- A CEO? Sky's the limit.

Despite those modest public salaries, politicians end up richer than CEOs. Although this girl I spoke about had a majority of her family in politics, she could still afford to study at an IB school. The question is: How did her family earn so much money?

The answer:

- Contract cuts (40% is the new 10%);
- Real estate scams;
- Cash-for-tickets;
- Cash-for-questions;
- The golden goose: Unaccounted 'election donations'.

I am using the girl as an example for almost all politicians. She may not be 'that' corrupt, perhaps nor is her family. These politicians aren't public servants. They've made the public their servants. Most of their wealth? Not even in their names. It's in the names of spouses, cousins, obscure NGOs, or their driver's nephew's shell company registered at one shady address in Nagpur or Rae Bareli.

My suggestion: The way to alleviate this problem and get good, educated, value-oriented patriotic youth to take up this service is to increase salaries and make this a viable profession to alleviate this problem and attract good, educated, value-oriented patriotic youth to this service, and establish some fast-track courts to hear the cases against politicians.

However, the larger problem for us is that Netas are always fundraising. Not for policy. But for re-election. The solution is simple. Ironically, Nehru introduced it. One nation. One election. Today, his party is opposing it. If politicians keep campaigning and trying to impress voters, when will they govern?

To impress us, they have now institutionalized bribery. They make promises to give money to unemployed youth or women, and if somehow, they can't buy you out… There are two opium bottles that never go out of fashion: Religion and something called ideology. We have discussed how left and right are decorative terms, but let me give you a few examples that you can use to question people with strong right and left beliefs.

The Bhartiya Janta Party or BJP is labelled right wing. By the traditional Western or American definition, that would mean low government intervention, pro-market capitalism, and individual freedom over collective welfare.

But in reality? They support massive welfare schemes (free rations, LPG cylinders, housing subsidies). They embrace state control in key sectors like defence, railways, and digital infrastructure. They champion protectionist economics, Make in India, import restrictions, and Foreign Direct Investment (FDI) scrutiny, all of which lean left on the global spectrum.

The Indian National Congress or INC is to be liberal and left. By Western standards, that would mean expansive welfare programmes, strong labour protections, a cautious approach to open markets and big business.

But what have they actually done?

- Introduced economic liberalization in 1991, breaking away from decades of socialist planning.
- Welcomed FDI, allowing global companies' deep entry into Indian markets.
- Dismantled licence-raj barriers and opened key industries from telecom to insurance in classic free-market fashion.

So, while the INC may project itself as a socially inclusive, welfare-minded party, economically, it executed one of the most capitalist turns in India's post-independence history.

So, who's right?

Who's left?

Honestly… who's even reading?

I hope you are. :D

However, economics is not what some will say defines right

and left in our country.

My dear educated politicians, let's go to your fountainheads:

- Nehru dreamed of secular socialism
- Hedgewar wanted a Hindu nation

But today, it is vending-machine leadership. Push a button to get whichever ideology suits the moment. Most jump ship. Switch scarves. Change parties like phone covers.

Closer home, our Member of Parliament started in one party when he was in his mid-twenties, and became the youngest Union Cabinet Minister, thanks to his lineage. But from 2014 to 2023, he stayed out of power and perhaps tried joining the BJP, failed, I think, and then joined a BJP ally instead. Why?

Power. Position. Relevance. I don't know. But one must ask to uncover this mask.

Fun fact: Over half the elected representatives in the BJP were once in the Congress.

Now they scream anti-national across the aisle at… themselves. That's not loyalty. That's not ideology.

There are exceptions:

Subramanian Swamy: Controversial, but consistent;

Shashi Tharoor: Thoughtful, articulate, and ideologically intact.

My suggestion: Switching parties should not be allowed more than once.

And if they can't divide you on ideology, the easiest weapon is invoking god.

They Instagram him. They tweet his blessings. They do photo-ops with folded hands and captions like 'Jai X, Jai Y, Jai Viral Engagement'.

Religion in politics? It works. It gives you:

- A cause you don't need to explain;
- An enemy you don't need to name;
- A distraction you don't need to clean up.

While they speak of places of worship, let's talk numbers. India has an estimated 7.5 lakh active temples, 300,000 plus active mosques, and 35,000 plus active churches. On average, all religious places host fifty plus people daily, often many more.

In contrast to our schools. We may have fourteen lakh schools, but:

- 35% of schools have fewer than fifty students.
- Many schools have no toilets, no electricity, and no teachers.

Let that sink in. We have more religious places filled with 50-plus people praying than schools with 50-plus children learning.

We build statues taller than skyscrapers, but can't build classrooms with roofs.

We put religion in every budget, but education is on the back bench.

Why? Because children don't vote. Gods somehow do.

To the best of my knowledge:

Ram didn't rally. Allah didn't campaign. Buddha didn't debate on TRPs. Jesus didn't file nominations.

And yet, today, god has become a campaign strategy, a communal provocation, a vote bank's most loyal ambassador. If there's a god, he's probably more interested in whether we feed the hungry, educate the children, and protect the vulnerable.

But that's not vote-catching material.

Hate is louder. Faith is easier to weaponize.

Religion has been reduced to a poll promise and how one religious community is going to capture the other... Hindu versus Muslim becomes the most potent and evergreen poison.

My suggestion is that all politicians should not be allowed to display religious beliefs during an election. Radical? Yes. Needed much? I think so.

Now, because of the state of our Neta and the barriers to entering politics, what is the state of our Parliament? The average age of our nation is twenty-eight. Lok Sabha's average age is fifty-four. The Rajya Sabha's average age is sixty-three.

This same Lok Sabha statistic in 1997 stood at an average age of 46.4. India is getting younger, but its politicians are getting older. Unsurprisingly, the youth are disinterested.

Meanwhile:

- Sanna Marin became Finland's PM at 34;
- Emmanuel Macron in France at 39;
- Jacinda Ardern in New Zealand at 37.

Some Indian politicians are older than Google, the internet, and in a few cases, the Constitution itself. Yes, age doesn't always mean disconnect. Modi. Gandhi. Perhaps ten of them get it. But put a Gen Alpha teen in a room with a 75-year-old MP and ask them to talk about AI, cancel culture, or Taylor Swift: You'll need subtitles.

Our policymaking? Buffering in 2G while the world runs on 5G. I don't blame our young for disillusionment; it's challenging to keep going, especially if you don't want to sell your beliefs or your neutrality.

At 23, I believed young people could push India into the UN Security Council. We rallied in 50-plus cities. I got 1,00,000 plus signatures. Walked with 10,000 plus people in Mumbai. Made it our agenda at every I.I.M.U.N. Conference. We got everyone, from Chief of RSS Mohan Bhagwat, to filmmaker Rohit Shetty to talk about this cause.

Just when we were about to host another event at the UN in 2017… India's Permanent Representative to the UN pulled the plug. Why? Because we didn't fit the narrative, we weren't 'useful'. He wasn't getting anything from us, perhaps. We complained and requested everyone.

Not a single politician helped.

We were kids. No references. Why would they?

Even today, our work in 100-plus cities has received no recognition from any government, state or centre. The now-retired Indian Ambassador to the UN was called to represent India's position to the world in our war against terrorism.

However, there is a silver lining; young MPs, once a part of I.I.M.U.N., were also called to serve. But they are now part of the system, so that they can be trusted.

The organization? Being neutral is inconvenient.

Leaders who vote tomorrow aren't worth engaging today.

Having seen how helpful public servants are and everything we discussed so far, I know why only less than 25% of eligible first-time voters turned out to vote.

But I haven't given up hope, because the 20-year-old girl who failed her engineering exams, suffered mental health issues, graduated from NYU, worked at the United Nations, then realized it is a puppet in the hands of the United States of America, has now started working in the US government. Kashvi's story, found in my book *Nothing But The Truth*, is why I believe there is hope.

We may not be able to change the creature, but we can stop them from controlling us. A politician's most significant power is controlling the narrative, from building a road to the movies we watch; they want to influence everything in this country. My suggestion is:

1. Clean Up Your Feed

Your algorithm isn't your ally. It doesn't show you the truth. It shows you your truth, again and again, until you believe that's the only one. That's not education. That's indoctrination.

Follow people across the spectrum. Read things that challenge you. Fact-check before forwarding. Listen before labelling.

Don't just be a content consumer. Be a context creator.

2. Call Out Shallow Patriotism

If someone says, 'How dare you question the government?' Ask them, 'How dare the government stop us from questioning?'

Questioning isn't anti-national. It's the most national thing you can do.

Blind obedience isn't love for your country. It's laziness in tricolour. Real patriotism is in building, questioning, staying here, not going abroad, and making people aware, even when it's inconvenient.

3. Vote. And Vote Better

Don't vote out of habit. Don't vote out of family tradition. Don't vote because a politician quoted your favourite god or did an interview with an influencer. Vote for:

- Those who show up;
- Those who answer questions;
- Those who remember what a manifesto is after the selfie is taken.

And yes, vote every time.

4. Build Your Own Narrative

You don't have to become a politician. But you must be politically aware, not in party colours, but in purpose. Start a movement.

Join a forum. Run for your college council. Intern in a ward office. Understand your rights. Read the Constitution, not just the Instagram post version.

Don't just post democracy. Practice it. Because silence isn't neutrality. It's permission.

Maybe the real question isn't, *who's the Neta of my narrative?* Maybe it's why we gave *up our narrative in the first place?*

Politics isn't just about the Parliament. It's about people who shape how we live, learn, love, and leave behind legacies. And no, they're not all evil. They're not all saints, either. They're just people, like you and me, responding to the systems we have created, the incentives we've built, the apathy we've enabled, and the cynicism we've normalized.

We keep saying, 'Politics is dirty.' Dirt doesn't clean itself. Someone has to get their hands dirty. Maybe you won't join a party. Maybe you'll never contest an election. But maybe, just maybe, you'll begin asking better questions; from your leaders, your friends, yourself. From that one super radical uncle, who knows everything that will happen before it happens.

Because democracy isn't just a vote, it's a habit, and it's formed… not once every five years, but in the way we think, speak, act, and show up. Daily.

The truth is, we don't need better politicians. We need better participation. That, my friend, starts with you.

It is time you became the Neta of your own narrative!

God's Plan... or Ours?

8.

As we've established in the last chapter, politics in India isn't just played on the ground; it's played in the name of the gods above. So, it's only right that we explore who god is.

Most of us were introduced to god before we could spell our names. Before we learnt how to think critically, we were told to fold our hands. Before we could ask *why*, we were told, 'He is watching. '

God was everywhere, in our victories (thank god I passed), in our failures (god is testing you), in fear (don't lie, god sees everything), in food (say grace), and even when someone gives birth to a child (*bhagwan ki kripa se hua!*).

Here's the thing. We're told to pray, but never told to question who we're praying to. We're told to believe in his books, his rules, his words, but never taught to think for ourselves.

Belief is handed down, not thought through. Obedience is rewarded. Doubt is punished.

Perhaps that's where it begins, our relationship with god, formed in fear, reinforced by culture, and rarely, if ever, investigated by the self.

In India, god is more than god. He is a voter magnet, a campaign poster, a rallying cry. We build temples before schools. We debate beef more than budget. Our films can't show kissing scenes, but if a character wears a sacred thread incorrectly, all hell breaks loose (sometimes literally). We scream 'Jai Shri Ram' in stadiums and on streets, but also in courtrooms and during lynchings.

Political parties from every spectrum have used God as a branding agency, rebranding their power as divine sanction.

Then there's everyday life. Whenever something terrible happens, a flood, an exam result, a breakup, we're told to pray. Go to the mandir, the dargah, the church, the gurdwara. Light a diya, tie a thread, say a mantra, shed a tear.

But rarely do we ask:

- Is there god? And if so, is this god listening? Or am I talking to myself?
- If a god exists, is he the one who asked for marble shrines and monetary offerings?
- Did god create religion? Or did religion create god?
- If there is no god, how did the universe build itself?

Then come the more complex questions, the ones we avoid because they shake the foundations:

- If god is all-knowing, why does he need us to tell him what we want?
- If he's all-powerful, why does suffering exist at such a scale, even in places of worship?
- If religion is meant to unite, why has it divided us more than anything else?

Finally, the one that silences most rooms: If god truly lives in all of us, why do we look for him everywhere else?

Let's face it, every religion claims a different god/s, a different heaven, a different hell, and a different moral code. In Jainism, even harming a microbe can trap you in karmic rebirths. In Islam, animal sacrifice is divine. In Christianity, confession cleanses sin. In Buddhism, there's no eternal soul to begin with. Who's right? More importantly, can they all be?

The books that delineated religion and made god? Are these holy books actually 'holy'?

Are they authored texts, written by men (almost always men) who lived in a specific time, had a particular worldview, and interpreted 'divine' experiences the only way they could?

Why is it that these books, supposedly eternal, often reflect the social hierarchies, misogyny, and power structures of their time?

And if they were truly from god, shouldn't they sound the same?

Here's what this section and this chapter will do:

It won't give you definitive answers. But it will give you questions. Because that's where your tryst with truth should begin. Not fear, but curiosity.

And just so we're clear…

⚠ Trigger Warning:

What you're about to read may offend your inherited beliefs. Not because it's blasphemous, but because it's different from what is conventionally acceptable. If you're willing to explore, read on. If not, you're free to skip ahead and continue outsourcing your truth. :D

Before I started questioning faith, religion, and the idea of god, I was exactly the kind of child every religious parent would be proud of. Born into a Gujarati Jain family, I didn't just recite the Namokar Mantra; I did it with complete sincerity. Twice a day. Once before bed. Once, right after waking up. Like brushing my teeth, but for my soul.

My mother still says, with pride in her voice, '*Maro dikro toh ghano dharmik hato.* (My son was very religious.)'

At the age of five, I climbed Shikharji, one of Jainism's holiest pilgrimage sites. I was proud. Not just because I'd done something difficult, but because I'd done something that made me feel, even if just for a moment, closer to something higher.

Something pure. Something divine.

I believed in heaven and hell. I believed Jainism was my moral compass, identity, and answer sheet. All my friends in school had their own gods, too. Different names, different faces, but all united by one thing: faith.

To be honest, back then, we weren't as interested in the gods as much as we were in the sweets. We shared laddoos during Ganesh Chaturthi and kheer during Baisakhi. God was cool, sure, but prasad was the real unifier.

Apart from religion, another thing my parents encouraged me for, was to read. I loved it. I was a classic nerd. I became a voracious reader.

History. Biographies. Scriptures. Science. Even Encyclopaedias. This became my favourite play date. One book, in particular, became a turning point: *My Experiments with Truth* by Mahatma Gandhi.

In it, he wrote a line that cracked open something inside me, 'At first, I thought God is Truth. Later, I realized Truth is God.'

That hit me. Not like thunder. More like a gentle nudge that keeps growing louder with time. Until then, I thought praying harder meant being closer to god. But Gandhi was saying: Don't just pray. Investigate. Experiment. Seek the truth, and in doing that, you'll find god. That idea didn't make me not believe in god. It made me curious. I didn't reject god. I just stopped accepting him blindly. From the age of 12 to 25, I drifted. I wasn't hostile to religion. I just wasn't… interested.

Other things took over; school, social life, hormones, ambition, heartbreak, hope. I read everything, but religion. God was like an old friend you once sat next to in class, familiar but no longer part of your daily life. The only time I would remember him would be before anything crucial would happen or when I fell ill.

Then, at 25, life handed me something deeply personal. I won't go into the specifics here, because what happened isn't the point. What shifted is. That moment brought me back to the big questions.

Not just 'Why did this happen?' but 'What lies beyond what I can see?'

I began again. This time, not as a child reciting mantras, but as an adult reading everything I could. The *Bhagavad Gita*, the *Bible*, the *Quran*, the *Dhammapada*, the *Guru Granth Sahib*, Jain *Agamas*, then the *Vedas* and *Upanishads*, and their many interpretations. I read religion, atheism, philosophy, and physics, and I even read a few 'God for Dummies' books in between.

Some books inspired me. Others infuriated me. But every book added another layer to the inquiry. And yet, through all of this, I must say this: my parents never stopped believing.

Our home still has idols, mantras playing softly in the background, pujas on auspicious days, and fasts observed with quiet reverence. They believe. Deeply. Unshakably. They love me irrespective of my crazy experiments. I am lucky that in some households, this would not be permitted. But I believe in something else, in the freedom to seek. The freedom to not inherit your truth, but to discover it. To challenge what you were told as a child, not out of disrespect, but out of responsibility to your own mind.

In that space, somewhere between the Namokar Mantra and Nietzsche, between temples and telescopes, I began building my own understanding of god, not as someone in the sky, but as a question worth pursuing. And my most burning one was? Where did it all begin?

Not just life. Not just humanity. But everything. Time. Space. Matter. Energy. Consciousness.

Science, of course, has its theory, the Big Bang. Roughly 13.8 billion years ago, all the matter and energy in the universe were compressed into a singularity, a point so dense that it defied comprehension. And then, bang. Expansion. Light. Atoms. Galaxies. Life.

It's elegant. It's mathematically sound. It's also, if we're being honest, incomplete.

Here's what science still can't answer:

- What came before the Big Bang?
- What caused that singularity to exist in the first place?
- And who or what, if anything, lit the fuse?

This is where my best friend, Anjani, often steps in with a confident smile and says,

'God did it.' Maybe that's true.

But then comes the counter-question: Did god create the universe? Or did the universe create god, as a story we told ourselves to make sense of the infinite?

That question might make some uncomfortable. But truth doesn't exist to comfort you. It exists to challenge you.

Every religion, every culture, every civilisation has tried to answer the same terrifying, humbling question. Unlike many texts that pretend to know it all, the *Rig Veda* opens with radical honesty. In the Nasadiya Sukta (10.129), it says:

Then even nothingness was not, nor existence…

The Gods came later than this world's creation, so who knows?

This isn't mythology. It's existential curiosity.

In the Vedic worldview:

- There is no start or stop, only cycles of appearance and disappearance.
- Truth isn't a person or a power, it's a lived experience of oneness.
- And god? Not someone to fear. But maybe something you already are.

After the Vedic era came the vast landscape of Hindu cosmology, filled with gods, timelines, avatars, and stories. Here, the universe:

- Is cyclical, created, sustained, and dissolved endlessly.
- Is measured in kalpas, yugas, and manvantaras.
- Runs on divine roles: Brahma, the creator; Vishnu, the preserver; Shiva, the destroyer.

One day of Brahma is equal to 4.32 billion years. After which, he sleeps. Then it starts again, much like yet another season of the sitcom *Friends*.

In Jainism, there's no creator at all. The universe just *is*. Always was. Always will be. God doesn't run the show; karma and causality do.

Islam takes a direct, structured approach:

- Allah created the universe in six stages.
- Humans were shaped from clay.
- The world is governed by divine will, law, and ultimate accountability.

It's a universe with clear authorship, order, and outcome. Submission isn't a weakness; it's alignment with the Creator's design.

And yes, Christianity has a similar beginning, 'Let there be light!' but with a different narrative, sin, salvation, and a returning saviour. Remember that guy called Jesus?

The Buddha was different; he never answered how the world began and didn't think it mattered. Why? Because obsessing over the origin of creation is like arguing about who lit the match… while your house is on fire.

For Buddhists:

- The universe is cyclical but godless.
- Everything is governed by cause and effect, not divine will.
- You don't escape the cycle by prayer, but by awareness.

The question is, what do we do with these stories?

We respect them. We read them. We must also be willing to question them.

Because they're not identical. And if they all claim to be the truth, who's right?

Don't just have faith. Question it. Let's not forget that none of these religious texts were actually written by the gods. Krishna didn't write the *Bhagavad Gita*; Ved Vyasa did, and even that was compiled centuries after the events supposedly occurred.

Jesus never wrote the Bible; *his disciples did*, decades after his death, in different languages, for different audiences. The *Quran* was revealed to the Prophet Muhammad, but was written down and compiled later by his followers. The Jain *Agamas*? Transmitted orally for centuries before being written 500 years after Mahavira. The Buddhist scriptures? Passed down through chants, remembered and reshaped across councils.

Now ask yourself if a game of Chinese whispers can't hold its accuracy across ten people in one room, what are the odds that these messages, passed down over millennia through empires, editors, scribes, politics, and printing presses, are precisely what 'god wanted you to hear'?

Are you following divine instruction? Or are you obeying Matthew, Vyasa, or some monk who thought women were distracting and heaven was members-only? What are the rituals you are following? Where is this energy being redirected?

Because at some point, it's not god you're worshipping. It's someone's edited version of god.

That brings me to a quote from one of my favourite philosophers, Friedrich Nietzsche: 'Faith means not wanting to know what is true.'

Here's what I've realized: 'The journey to the discovery of truth is rejecting what is false and therefore, let me share what I think is false.'

First, for all believers, allow me to show you a few absolute inconsistencies that exist, thereby showing you why religion as it exists today, is false.

Hinduism (Post-Vedic)

Take the *Manusmriti*, often cited as the moral-legal backbone of dharma:

'A Shudra should serve the other three castes; that is his highest dharma.' (*Manusmriti* 1.91)

But the *Bhagavata Purana*, revered across sects and temples, says, 'The Supreme Lord resides more in the heart of the humble and lowly devotee than in ritualistic offerings.' (*Bhagavata Purana* 1.9.27)

So, which is it?

Are caste divisions an eternal law? Or is devotion the great equalizer?

You can't say god lives in everyone and then gatekeep god based on birth. Similarly, the *Skanda Purana* condemns meat-eating: 'He who eats meat will be eaten in the next life by the same creature.' (*Skanda Purana* 2.2.42.15)

But the *Kalika Purana prescribes animal sacrifice:* 'The goat, when killed in sacrifice, goes to heaven… thus meat is not impure.' (*Kalika Purana* 8.20)

Is purity defined by the animal, or the intention behind the knife?

The beauty of this religion is that the very texts that they claim their basis on, the Vedas, have no mention of the words Hindu or Hinduism in them!

Jainism

Jainism stands firm on *Ahimsa*, non-violence, toward all living beings, no exceptions.

'A true monk does not cause injury to plants, seeds, insects, or fire.' (*Acharanga Sutra* 1.1.5)

Then comes Sallekhana, the ritual of fasting unto death, praised in the *Tattvartha Sutra*: 'Sallekhana is welcomed when the body is no longer useful for spiritual advancement.' (*Tattvartha Sutra* 7.22)

If killing even bacteria is violence, how is self-starvation a virtue? If renunciation is ideal, why are Jain temples some of the most extravagant structures in India?

Islam

Don't get me started.

The Quran proclaims, 'There is no compulsion in religion.' (Surah Al-Baqarah 2:256)

It also commands, 'If they turn back, seize them and kill them wherever you find them.' (Surah An Nisa 4:89)

'Those who disbelieve, their abode shall be the fire; they shall dwell therein forever.' (Surah Al-Baqarah 2:39)

Is faith a choice or a command? Allah is described as 'Most Merciful, Most Compassionate'.

Which version of god are we meant to believe?

On gender, Islam says, 'Men are the protectors and maintainers of women.' (Surah An-Nisa 4:34)

'The testimony of a woman equals half that of a man.' (Surah Al-Baqarah 2:282)

What happened to all the Muslim women fighting for women's empowerment? Do you believe in empowerment, or do you believe in Islam?

Christianity

Jesus says, 'Love your enemies and pray for those who persecute you.' (Matthew 5:44)

The Old Testament says, 'Do not spare them; put to death men, women, children, and infants.' (Samuel 15:3)

Which god are we supposed to believe, the forgiving father or the vengeful warrior?

On salvation, Christianity says, 'Whoever believes in Him shall not perish but have eternal life.' (John 3:16)

Also, 'Faith without works is dead.' (James 2:26)

So, is heaven earned by belief or behaviour? My question is, does heaven or hell exist, or was the author as imaginative as Dante was?

Buddhism

The Buddha warned against clinging to rituals: 'Rites and rituals cannot lead to Nirvana.' (Majjhima Nikaya 2.2.5)

Yet modern Buddhist practice is full of incense offerings, bell ceremonies, chanting in elaborate temples and gold statues of a man who walked away from gold.

He taught detachment. But Vajrayana Buddhism teaches the symbolic use of deities, mantras, and visualizations, all built on mental engagement with form.

So, was Nirvana supposed to be found in silence, or surrounded by gold and gongs?

Let's stop pretending. These aren't religious paradoxes. They are absolute inconsistencies, contradictions that can't be brushed off with metaphor or context, and I say it having read the texts.

If these are god's words, why don't they match? If the message is eternal, why does it change verse to verse, book to book, in the same religion? Maybe god never contradicted himself. Or he did, because I believe he was just another human being, even if he had superhuman abilities. But the men who claimed to speak for him? They were contradictory, quite often, and without apology.

It's time we asked:

- Who edited these texts?
- Who benefits from the contradictions?
- And why is confronting them seen as sin, instead of sense?

Do you honestly believe god, the infinite, timeless, all-knowing creator of the cosmos, is sitting on a celestial throne, going, 'Hmm. Rishabh offered me only one coconut this week. Strike one.'

Or worse, 'He didn't build a temple in my name. Strike two.' If god exists, I highly doubt he's managing an Excel sheet of coconuts, camphor and collaterals he received. But somewhere along the way, religion has turned into a transaction.

God? He became the brand. Take India alone.

- Tirupati Temple rakes in over ₹3,000 crore a year.
- Padmanabhaswamy Temple is worth 1,20,000 crore; more

than the GDP of almost all North Eastern Indian states.

- Many temples have more gold than the Reserve Bank, without filing a single income tax return!

Meanwhile, outside those same temples, kids sell flowers instead of going to school. Devotees walk barefoot, not out of choice, but because they can't afford slippers and no one offers them a glass of that milk we pour over stone idols.

Do you want to impress god? Feed a hungry child. Don't flood a statue.

Have you ever seen a temple rate card? It's basically a restaurant menu.

- ₹501: Basic aarti;
- ₹1,100: Special puja;
- ₹5,001: Fast-track darshan;
- ₹25,000: Deluxe God combo; puja, prasad, VIP seating, and a selfie with the priest.

I'm sure soon there will be a ₹10 lakh 'God's inner circle' package, which comes with a spiritual blue tick and early access to moksha.

We say, 'God is everywhere.' Then we queue up for hours unless we've paid for the fast tag. Why? Is it a toll you are crossing? I did not know that salvation has Ola's surge pricing.

Then there's the great Indian export, the spiritual entrepreneur. They wear saffron, sometimes white, and live like CEOs. They endorse everything, from toothpaste to governments. They sell everything, from miracle water to customized karma detoxes. Some promise you'll find peace. We believe them.

Because when someone mixes Sanskrit with TED Talk energy and sprinkles in some vague quantum physics, we mistake charisma for enlightenment.

Spoiler alert: Ram did not ask for donations on Diwali. And just like Ram, I am certain neither did the others.

So why is a Guru building a 7-star ashram, making a statue of Shiva and then collecting donations in his name? Use common sense. If god wanted a palace, he wouldn't have been born in a cow shed. If he wanted gold, he wouldn't have walked barefoot. If he needed your money, well, he probably wouldn't be god.

I'm not against culture. I am against performance in the name of the divine.

We've turned temples into toll booths, priests into middlemen, and devotion into direct debit.

Then we wonder why the world feels hollow. I conclude my views on religion by agreeing with Karl Max, who said, 'Religion is the opium for the people'. And I will add, *'Because we could not produce enough opium, we created religion.'*

Let me be clear. I don't have a problem with god. I never had. In fact, I genuinely believe there were, and perhaps still are, individuals with extraordinary abilities. People who tapped into something deeper than intellect. Call them saints, avatars, mystics, or, in Marvel terms, superheroes.

I believe they were Avengers in real life, why is it hard to imagine that someone like Krishna lifted minds and mountains? But here's the problem.

We've confused admiration with deification. We took powerful humans, elevated their stories, and then built systems around them that those very people probably would have rejected. Imagine this.

Five thousand years from now, a curious civilisation stumbles upon videos of Amitabh Bachchan, intense, poetic, commanding respect from millions. They see recordings of Narendra Modi addressing stadiums, influencing the fate of a billion people.

Would they call them gods? Probably. But does that make them divine? Or is it just profoundly influential?

That's what I believe happened with many of the 'gods' of the past. They may have been real. They may all have been searching for the truth. But they were still human, not to be worshipped unquestioningly, but studied, understood, and good parts emulated.

What began as reverence turned into religion. What began as wisdom became worship. What began as guidance got rewritten as law. We started following stories, not truths.

Rituals, not realizations. Priests, not presence.

So, then some of you may ask, 'What are your views on god?' Well, I don't know, and I don't claim to know.

But long before religion as we know it, India had a different idea, *Advaita Vedanta*, which I am no expert in, but which resonates in parts.

It didn't say 'obey god.' It said, 'You are That: Tat Tvam Asi.'

'Aham Brahmasmi: The Brahman alone is real. The world is an illusion.'

Aham Brahmasmi: I am Brahman. It wasn't arrogance. It was awareness. Not the English translation that you are the Supreme Being, but that the Supreme Being is not separate from you.

No temples. No labels. No fear. No monetary transactions.

Just a simple recognition, you are not just a body. You are not even just a mind. You are awareness itself. And no, it is not baba babble; Quantum physics today talks of:

- Particles being interconnected across galaxies;
- Your observations shaping reality;
- Consciousness as a possible building block of the universe.

Some call it simulation theory. Others call it unified field theory. Or just call it what sages called it centuries ago, Brahman.

What you see is not the whole picture. What you feel, that stillness behind all thought, might just be the closest we've ever come to oneness.

I don't reject god. To be clear, I don't accept him either. I learn the good things from his stories.

I reject the business that is now called religion. What I also definitely reject are the institutions built in his name.

If you ask me what to worship? I'll say, 'Don't worship. Or Do. That's your choice.'

I will tell you what I do. I don't worship. I try to be still. I try to be aware. I observe. And occasionally, while observing, I doze off. Haha!

So here we are. Not at the end of a sermon. Not at the gates of heaven. Just at the end of a chapter. And maybe, the beginning of a deeper question.

Everything you've just read? It's my truth as I see it *today*. Crafted through years of doubting, reading, my closest friends eye-rolling me, temple-hopping, overthinking, under-praying, and just quietly watching the world.

Your truth? That's up to you to find. Because this isn't a subscription plan. You don't have to 'agree' to continue. You just have to stay curious. So please, whatever you do:

Don't believe something just because it's old. Don't fear something just because it's wrapped in ritual. Truth doesn't wear robes. It doesn't beg to be followed. It sits quietly, waiting for you to ask better questions.

Like, 'Does this even make sense?'

Or like, 'Does this chapter even make sense?'

If the answer's yes, follow it. If the answer's no, challenge it. If the answer is I don't know, smile. That's where truth begins.

Hotter than Your Ex's DM: Planet Earth

9.

You've probably heard the words 'climate change' so often that it's started sounding like elevator music in a shopping mall, always playing in the background, never really noticed. A phrase floating around in debates, news tickers, and maybe a random school project titled 'Save Earth' with a blue-and-green drawing and a sad polar bear.

But let's not kid ourselves. This isn't background noise anymore. In this story, it's the main character. And the climax is closer than you think.

We all want to build a *Viksit Bharat* by 2047; a nation that's prosperous, respected, and rising. But here's a truth bomb: if we don't act now, our 100-year celebration may come with oxygen cylinders, water rations, and tomatoes at ₹800 per kg.

And if you think that's not going to happen, I'll let data speak for itself:

- The Intergovernmental Panel on Climate Change (IPCC) warns South Asia could warm by 2.2°C to 2.7°C by 2047 if emissions continue unchecked.
- According to the Asian Development Bank (ADB), India may lose 2.5% of its GDP annually due to climate-related disasters by 2050.
- Over 160 million Indians living in coastal zones could be impacted by rising sea levels.
- Himalayan glaciers, the source of our major rivers, are melting at record speeds, threatening water supply for over 600 million people. The World Bank estimates that by 2030, 40%

of Indians may not have reliable access to drinking water.

- Globally, 1.2 billion people could become climate refugees by 2050, many from regions like ours.

This isn't about saving penguins. It's about whether your city will be breathable in ten years. If you're reading this from an Indian metro, I needn't tell you more. It's about whether your kids will know what a mango tastes like in summer. It's about whether you'll even be able to step outside without a pollution mask and a weather warning.

Some may argue, 'But bro, isn't the earth always changing?' Sure. Earth's climate has undergone significant changes over millions of years. Not at this pace. Not this unnaturally.

Definitely not because of us.

To all the non-believers who say things like:

- Climate change is a hoax: Ask the 20 million people displaced by floods in Pakistan or farmers watching crops die under unseasonal rains in Vidarbha. Hoaxes don't destroy homes.
- Earth heals itself: True, but earth needs time. Right now, we're breaking more than she can bandage.
- It's just a phase: So was the Ice Age. Do you want to go back to that, bro?
- We need development, so this is collateral damage: Okay, but what's the use of eight-lane highways if your kids are stuck indoors with asthma and heatstroke?

This isn't a future problem. It's not just something affecting tree-huggers or lab-coat scientists. It's not something we can meme away.

Climate change is happening. Please don't say, 'Drill, baby, drill.'

In 2025, climate change is no longer theoretical; it's unfolding across India in real time:

- Record heatwaves gripped north India, with Barmer, Rajasthan, hitting 46.4°C and over 170 reported heatstroke cases.
- Assam's Dhemaji district faced severe floods, displacing families and causing long-term migration.
- Himalayan glaciers are retreating rapidly, threatening downstream water supplies.
- Telangana's groundwater levels remained critically low despite above-average rainfall in April 2025.
- Crop damage in Bihar affected mangoes, lychees, and wheat due to scorching pre-harvest heat.
- Ahmedabad launched urban cooling measures, including reflective roofs and misting bus stops, to protect low-income residents.

These aren't future fears, they're present-day facts.

Imagine this: It's 2047. India has turned 100. But instead of people bicycling in eco-cafes, we're battling a climate crisis that slipped through our fingers while we scrolled.

Aira lives in Pune, or what's left of it. She's forty-five now, a working professional and parent who grew up in the pre-climate emergency era, when weather apps didn't come with health warnings. Her teenage daughter has never seen snow. She knows glaciers from textbooks and YouTube clips, not trekking trips. Their annual family vacation? Cancelled. Forest fires in Himachal shut down most tourist spots. Again. Aira checks an app tracking oxygen levels before sending her daughter to school, like people once checked traffic. She carries three masks in her handbag:

one for air pollution, one for dust storms, and another because COVID-19 never fully disappeared.

She shops weekly, not for groceries, but for bottled drinking water. Rice is heavily rationed. Ration cards have returned, QR-coded and geo-tracked. She works hybrid, not by choice but because stepping outside more than an hour in summer risks heatstroke. Air quality hasn't dipped below hazardous in seventeen days straight. Some days, there's no running water. On others, the basement floods.

Aira once tried a climate-tech venture to help housing societies track energy use. It never launched. Investors pulled out, citing environmental volatility. She hasn't given up; she volunteers monthly at her daughter's school, runs upcycling workshops, and coordinates rainwater harvesting via a local WhatsApp group. She still believes it's not too late, just dangerously close.

Welcome to India @ 100. This could be reality if we don't act now. If it sounds dystopian, it's because it is. Yet, it's not fiction. It's forecast.

- Summers will regularly exceed 50°C in metros like Delhi, Ahmedabad, and Nagpur.
- Mumbai and Chennai will face annual urban flooding; coastal erosion will consume entire localities.
- Vector-borne diseases like dengue and chikungunya will reach the Himalayas.
- Heatwaves will kill thousands, especially vulnerable populations.
- Climate anxiety-driven mental health crises will rise sharply. Indian actor Bhumi Pednekar discussed her climate anxiety issues at an I.I.M.U.N. event in 2025. Just imagine the number of people experiencing this by 2047.
- Water wars between Indian states will dominate the news.

- Air pollution will be year-round, not seasonal.

This isn't to scare you; it's to wake you up. What we're heading towards isn't an apocalypse.

It's an avoidable disaster.

The Final Exam of Our Generation

Everyone talks about board exams. Competitive exams. UPSC. But this? This is the real test.

No grace marks. No retests. By 2047, you will inherit either a thriving nation or one merely surviving. The climate doesn't care about GDP or manifestos. It reacts only to emissions, inaction, and excuses.

So before planning smart cities, let's ensure there's a liveable planet to build them. Before toasting to Viksit Bharat, let's ensure Bharat is still standing.

Fortunately, environmental sustainability has been part of our DNA since recorded history.

Our original gods weren't kings; they were the sun, wind, and earth. The *Rig Veda*, one of the world's oldest texts, starts not with a god on a throne, but with Agni, the fire god. It invokes Vayu (wind), Varuna (water), Surya (sun), and Prithvi (earth), forces of nature worshipped as sacred energy.

The *Atharva Veda's Prithvi Sukta*, perhaps the world's oldest environmental poem, honours Mother Earth's generosity and balance:

The Earth, in which lie the ocean, rivers, and other waters, in which food and cornfields have come to be... may she confer on us the finest of her harvests.

This isn't a prayer for wealth. It's a prayer for sustainability. Our sustainability via her.

Indian philosophy centres on the five elements: Earth (Prithvi), water (Apas), fire (Agni), air (Vayu), and space (Akasha). Our bodies, minds, and environments all reflect these elements. Polluting nature is equivalent to polluting yourself. Now, that's something worth putting in a school textbook.

But how many of us ever read that growing up?

We often hear *Bharat Mata ki Jai*. But before becoming a symbol of political pride, she was *Bhoomi Devi*, the Earth goddess. In Indian thought, *Dharti Maa* isn't a metaphor; it's a literal truth. We touched the ground before rising. Ask a tree's permission before plucking a flower. Gave up food during festivals, not for detox fads, but for ecological balance.

And cutting down a tree? That was called *adharma*, a moral failing. Long before Greta Thunberg, Indian women embraced trees literally:

The Chipko Movement in the 1970s saw villagers hugging trees to stop deforestation.

That wasn't activism, it was affection. Proof that Indians never needed reminders to love the earth. We remembered. We revered. We reduced. We reused.

So, What Went Wrong?

Colonial industrial models taught us to see nature as a resource, to extract, exploit, and export. Then came concrete jungles. Air-conditioned malls. A culture of convenience. And somewhere along the way, the sacred became saleable.

The same country that revered rivers now faces dire water pollution. As of 2025, over 100 billion litres of untreated sewage are discharged daily into rivers like the Yamuna and Hindon, declared 'dead' or hugely toxic.

We build eco-resorts, clearing protected forest land. India has lost over 2.33 million hectares of tree cover since 2000, with 95% wiped from natural forests. We host green summits where every attendee gets a plastic water bottle. India generates approximately 26,000 tonnes of plastic daily, much of which ends up in landfills or nature due to poor recycling.

Our Biggest Cultural Exports Today Include:

- Festivals that choke water bodies: Despite eco-friendly efforts, non-biodegradable idol immersion during Ganesh Chaturthi pollutes lakes and rivers. And what about the Kumbh Mela?
- Weddings that emit as much carbon as a small village: Lavish Indian weddings produce 45,000 to 60,000 kg CO_2, equal to flying 150 people round-trip from Delhi to Dubai.
- The IPL (yes, ironically, I watch it too!) spans multiple cities with massive carbon emissions: A single IPL match in 2023 emitted ~10,000 tonnes CO_2e, comparable to over two million homes' daily emissions. Over a full season, emissions reach 750,000 to 900,000 tCO_2e, a stark rise from 42,264 tCO_2e estimated in 2010.

Then there's corporate India, launching flashy sustainability campaigns while quietly deforesting thousands of hectares for factories, mines, and roads.

We're not alone in this hypocrisy. But we should know better.

Meanwhile, the West's Contribution:

Europe and North America have caused nearly 50% of cumulative carbon emissions since the Industrial Revolution. India and most of Africa account for less than 5% historically, yet suffer the worst.

They industrialized. They profited. Now, they moralize.

Even their pop culture pollutes:

- In 2023, Taylor Swift's private jet emitted over 8,000 metric tonnes of CO_2: 1,200 times more than an average person.
- At Coachella, over 100,000 people flew in, burning jet fuel, dancing under diesel-powered lights in a desert where water must be imported.

They don't just consume, they export consumption as culture; fast fashion, single-use everything, streaming at scale. It's climate-neutral as long as the branding says so.

Climate change is colonialism 2.0, but now, the resource being looted is survival itself.

Global Climate Summits: A Quick Tour (Or Canva Presentations with Chocolate Sprinkles)

1997: Kyoto Protocol: The world's first serious climate pact, supposed to be legally binding. The US signed, waved to cameras, then ghosted. Canada pulled out. China and India had no binding targets.
Result? Many signatures, little action.

2009: Copenhagen Summit (COP15): Big promises, zero follow-through. 'A political accord' agreeing to 'maybe think about doing something someday.'

Climate: 0
Humans: 1

2015: Paris Agreement: Selfie sticks, hashtags, and custom pens ready. Countries set their own goals, with no penalties for failure. Now, most are off track, heading for a 2.7°C rise.

2021:COP26, Glasgow: Same story.

2023: COP28, Dubai: This was held in a petrostate and chaired by an oil CEO. It's like inviting a mosquito to lead a malaria awareness camp. Don't forget Davos, the biggest party! Results? The same, so no need to go into detail. In all these global gatherings, terms changed like trends: MDGs. SDGs. Net Zero by 2070. Net Maybe by 2100.

Next up: Carbon-Neutral Vibes Only.

As Greta Thunberg said (and I quote), 'Blah blah blah.'

The problem isn't just policy… It's psychology.

Why did it come to this? Because we treat nature as a sideshow, not the main character. We see climate as someone else's problem. We confuse greenwashing with green action.

So, where do we go from here? Saving the world doesn't mean you must become a coconut-sipping minimalist in a solar-powered forest hut, though if you can, that's awesome.

But for most of us, you won't quit everything, move to a forest, and build a compost toilet. But guess what? You don't need to.

Saving the planet isn't about perfection; it's about small tweaks with big impact. You don't need to be flawless. Just slightly less reckless.

Here are some things you can do to take your bit:

1. Eat local. Eat seasonal.

Not because a wellness influencer said so, but because your grandparents did.

Mangoes in summer, amla in winter, no blueberries imported from five continents away. This reduces transport emissions and supports local farmers.

2. Refuse fast fashion. Buy wisely.
You don't need twelve new outfits for twelve Instagram posts. No threats from the fashion police, but the planet will thank you. A question for brands: Are they truly eco-conscious or just greenwashing? Vote with your wallet. Buy less, but better.

3. Compost and segregate waste.
Leftovers don't belong in landfills; they need a second life. Peels → compost. Plastic → recycling. That bin you ignore? It's frontline climate action.

4. Plant trees, not excuses.
Trees are *shabda-rūpa devata*, living embodiments of the divine. Neem in your backyard, tulsi on your: green is the new godly.

5. Save water like a desert dweller.
Remember buckets over showers? That wasn't poverty, it was planet-saving. Maybe it's time to bring back the bucket and bucket your ego.

6. Use AI wisely.
Every Chat GPT question burns significant energy, 4–5 times more than a Google search. Training models use millions of kilowatt-hours, enough to power an Indian village for months. So while AI is cool and helpful, it's not carbon-neutral magic. The cloud runs on real electricity. Use tech, but use it wisely.

7. Speak up. Show up. Start small.
Discuss climate in your classroom, WhatsApp group, or building AGM. Join clean-ups. Volunteer. Plant trees that outlive you. Revolutions need consistency, not speeches.

8. Vote for climate-sensitive politicians.
Incremental effort helps, but big policy changes are essential.

9. Overconsumption: calm down, capitalism.
Half of the world's climate stress comes from wanting *more*. Do you really need seven serums and three almond-milk varieties? Minimalism isn't a trend; it's survival.

10. Don't order everything. Make an effort.
Every Zomato or Swiggy order fuels a delivery vehicle. Next time your city's smog blankets the sky, remember your role. Walk to the Kirana store instead; it helps your lungs and the city's too.

Even if I don't do all these, let's start with one. Remember, next time 'climate change' plays like elevator music, don't zone out. Because this isn't background noise anymore, it's the main character, remember?

Hustle, Happiness and the Holy Rupee

10.

Meet Mr Model Life.

Middle class. Studied hard. Took tuitions. Got 95%. Engineering. Placement. Decent package. Married someone from his caste. Bought a house. Bought a car. Had two kids (one 'artsy,' one 'studious'). Took two vacations. Retired at sixty. Now listens to bhajans. Talks about moksha. And is everyone's benchmark for 'how to live right'.

You've heard this story. You've been compared to this story. You may even be living this story.

Because society doesn't just teach us how to live; it hands us a blueprint. Like an AI toolkit, but for existence. (Ironically, AI can give you a toolkit for life, but that's another chapter.)

Study. Earn. Marry. Reproduce. Retire. Worship. Happiness will follow. Eventually.

And if you ever question this path? You're met with, '*Beta, Sharma ji ne toh itna accha settle kiya hai…*' But no one tells you that Sharma ji still doesn't sleep well.

'We have worked so hard to provide you this life.'

Yes, thank you, I really appreciate it, *but what about my happiness*?

What if happiness isn't a destination at 60, but a rhythm you choose at sixteen? What if the point isn't to 'settle down,' but to wake up?

We've been sold a one-size-fits-all story. But your life isn't a factory product. You're not a spreadsheet. You're a soul.

Let's ask the questions we were taught not to:

- What if hustling your way to a milestone is not what it's supposed to be?
- What if earning well isn't success but survival?
- What if happiness isn't a private jet and ten cars?
- What if retirement isn't rest but regret, if you never lived before it?

Now, here's a reality check:

- India's GDP per capita (2024): USD 2,700/year (~₹2.2L/year)
- India's Happiness Index Rank (2024): 126/143
(Ranked lower than Ukraine, Iraq, and Venezuela)

So, while the economy is 'rising,' our inner world is not. We're getting richer, but not necessarily wiser, freer, or more fulfilled.

To all the uncles and aunties, prescribing the model life, if the current definition of success worked, wouldn't we be… happier?

Also, here's a confession. I don't have all the answers. But thankfully, some of our ancestors did.

Let's address the hustle then. Long before 'hustle culture' became a hashtag, our scriptures, *our* Indian thought, offered a very different lens. And that's what I want to explore with you now.

I believe in hard work. The kind that makes your back sweat and your heart full. The kind that changes lives, not just increases likes on your LinkedIn posts. The kind you do for purpose, people, and progress, not applause.

But hustling? Hustling is not the same thing. Hustling is like lighting a diya in a storm and wondering why it keeps blowing out. It's effort without alignment, motion without meaning.

Not a service, but a scramble.

Hustle is when your worth depends on other people's validation. When rest feels illegal. And somewhere along the way, we confused this for virtue. But where did hustle culture even come from?

Let's trace its origins.

Hustle culture wasn't born in India. It was born in factories, in the West. The British brought it here during colonial rule. It suited their systems: predictable workers, fixed hours, and maximum output with minimum soul.

That's the blueprint we inherited. Now we debate between 70-hour and 90-hour work weeks.

What if I told you this was a pointless debate? Everything we observe comes from an imported lens. Have you ever wondered why Sunday is our default day of rest? That came from Abrahamic traditions, particularly Christianity, where Sunday is the Lord's Day.

The British made it official during their rule, not for *our* well-being, but for *their* factories.

But India? We didn't rest because a calendar told us to. We rested because the rhythm of life told us to. Ekadashi, Amavasya, Poornima, rest days aligned with the moon. Festivals, not just holidays, but pauses for joy, reflection, and gratitude.

We didn't work 9 to 5 and collapse on weekends. We worked with awareness and rested without guilt. Sometimes, seven days a week. Sometimes, none at all. Because it wasn't about the hours, it was about the intention. We didn't have 'grind culture'. We had *karma* and *seva*. We believed that work is sacred, not frantic; dharma is personal, not a societal checklist; service is an offering, not a branding opportunity.

From farming to teaching to creating art, you gave your best not to be 'seen,' but because it was the right thing to do. Our elders worked incredibly hard. But their energy was offering, not overcompensation.

They knew that the work done in awareness builds communities. Work done in panic burns people out. It's not the hustle that built ancient India. It was a responsibility. Relationship. Rhythm. Reverence.

As the *Rig Veda* reminds us:

Saṅgacchadhvaṁ saṁ vadadhvaṁ saṁ vo manāṁsi jānatām/
Devā bhāgaṁ yathā pūrve sañjānānā upāsate//

(Let us move together, speak together, let our minds be in harmony just as the gods once did.)

Real effort, in the Indian way, wasn't about being first. It was about moving forward, together. And how do you identify whether the work you are doing is full of purpose or hustle?

Would you return to work or study tomorrow if I gave you enough money to live comfortably?

If your answer is 'no,' then perhaps you are not working, you are hustling. I want to unequivocally be clear, this isn't an attack on ambition. We've built civilisations on the back of effort. But our tradition didn't teach us to chase. It taught us to contribute.

That's why our grandparents woke up before sunrise and fed the cows, the family, and the neighbours, before they ever thought of profit. That's why our teachers were called gurus, not just educators, because they gave knowledge as *daan*, not content as a commodity.

Hard work isn't new to India. What's new… is working without meaning. So no, I'm not saying don't work hard. I'm saying, work honestly. Work joyfully. Work meaningfully.

So if the Indian ideal wasn't *'rise and grind'* but *'rise and give,'* then here's the next big question: Give what? And in exchange for what?

Whether you're running a business, building a non-profit, or planning your next big pitch, you can't ignore it. The conversation will surround money. The one thing everyone wants. But no one is allowed to talk about it without being labelled greedy.

What *is* money, really?

Is it paper? A promise? Crypto coins? A reward for your time? Or a price for your soul?

Originally, money was simple. I have wheat. You have cloth. Let's trade.

Too complicated? Fine: Here's a coin. It stands for a particular exchange, so let's trade.

But today? Money is no longer just a medium of exchange. It's a marker of status, a measurement of success, a mirror for self-worth. We've turned it from means to meaning.

Today, money is:

- A UPI ping;
- A salary slip;
- A startup valuation;
- A family WhatsApp debate on 'Shaadi budget'.

We check our bank balances more than our reflections. We track our net worth more than our peace of mind. And somewhere in between:

- Survival was replaced by scale.
- Comfort was replaced by comparison.
- Need got confused with 'aesthetic' wants.

But wait, is wanting more money *a bad thing*? Not at all. Let's get this straight. Money is power. Money is freedom. Money is infrastructure, especially if you want to build, serve, or give. You can't run schools, movements, or homes on 'good intentions'.

So no, wanting money isn't wrong. But worshipping it blindly is.

Unlike many traditions that treat money as sinful, India never hated wealth.

In fact, we personified it.

- Lakshmi: The goddess of wealth, beauty, and abundance;
- Artha: One of the four *purusharthas* (goals of life), alongside *Dharma*, *Kama*, and *Moksha*.

We were told to earn honestly, use wisely, and detach gracefully. The real red flag wasn't wealth. It was *hoarding* without *offering*.

But how much is 'enough'? Let's flip the question: Would we still do what we're doing right now, if no one clapped and no one paid? If the answer is no, that's okay. But it means money is no longer a tool; it's our reason.

So 'enough' isn't a number. It's a mindset. A muscle. A decision not to let your entire life be priced.

Let's be honest. We're the generation that:

- Gets investment advice on Instagram;
- Obsessively checks stock apps;
- But still gets overwhelmed by Excel sheets.

We know how to transfer ₹10,000 in 10 seconds, but we don't know how to feel when we have ₹100 left at month-end. We chase six figures and then panic when we get them. Because no one told us that money doesn't fix meaning; it just funds it.

So, what should we do with the money? Use it.

- Use it to buy back your time.
- Use it to serve your community.
- Use it to build what you believe in.
- Use it so you never have to betray your values to make a living.

And most importantly: Earn with ethics. Spend with awareness. Give with joy. Because if money is your god, you'll always feel poor. But if money is your guest, you'll always stay rich. Besides, you've already read my views on god… 😄

So no, don't demonize money.

Let's hope the government never demonetizes it again as well.

Because the hardest thing to kill… isn't debt or desire; it's obsession.

Well, Kabir put it best:

Maya mari na man mara, mar mar gaya sharir
Asha trishna na mari, kahi gaye das Kabir.

(Desire didn't die, nor did the mind. The body withered away instead. Hope and greed still lived on, says Kabir.)

We've spoken about money, how we earn it, how we chase it. How we save it, spend it, flaunt it, and sometimes, lose ourselves to it.

But here's the truth:

Most people don't want money for money. They want what they *think* it will bring:

- A calmer breath;
- A lighter mind;
- A sense of being enough, finally.

And that, in a word, is happiness. Not the loud kind. Not the one found in applause or approval. But the one that sits silently in the room, when you're not performing for anyone.

What *is* happiness, then?

Is it a feeling? A reward? A practice? Something you unlock when life finally goes your way?

In Indian thought, happiness wasn't about intensity. It was about stability. It was not about a high, but about being held.

Science says happiness is chemicals. Dopamine when you finish a task or get a like. Serotonin is when you feel stable and connected. Oxytocin is released when someone hugs you. Endorphins are released when you exercise or laugh.

It's helpful to know how your brain works. But here's where it gets tricky:

These chemicals spike. They fade. They depend on something external.

And if we only rely on them, we start chasing the next thrill, the next item we didn't need to buy, or just one more episode. The cycle continues. In Indian philosophy, happiness wasn't something you chased. It was something you realigned with.

There were three key ideas:

- Sukha: Pleasure or comfort (temporary, sensory);
- Santosha: Contentment, peace with what is;
- Ananda: Bliss, your unchanging natural state.

Imagine this like:

- *Sukha* is an ice cream.
- *Santosha* is a quiet evening after a long day;
- *Ananda* is the sky that holds every season, unchanged, ever-present.

The goal wasn't to constantly feel good. It was to remain rooted, even when things didn't feel good. You've been told, 'Follow your passion, and you'll never work a day in your life.'

That sounds great until you realize even the things you love can feel heavy sometimes.

Writing, building, dancing, teaching, and even your *purpose* will demand rest, reflection, and repetition. And that's okay.

Real happiness isn't when life stops asking things of you. It's when you stop demanding perfection from life. Santosha doesn't mean you have no ambition. It means your peace isn't postponed until it's achieved. It's not the death of drive; it's the birth of discernment.

- You can grow without guilt.
- You can want more, without being hollow.
- You can show up fully, without showing off constantly.

Santosha is not settling. It's knowing what's worth settling for.

Ask yourself:

- What feels like peace, even when I'm tired?
- What makes me feel complete, not just busy?

So, maybe, happiness is…

- A dinner that no one clicks a picture of.
- A task done well, even if no one noticed.
- A friend who understands *before* you explain yourself.
- A morning where nothing significant happens, but your shoulders drop anyway.

Maybe happiness isn't found. Maybe it's remembered. Maybe it's not a reaction, but a return. And maybe the real flex isn't being endlessly excited. Maybe it's just being okay with where you are.

I didn't always think this way. I started out just like the version of 'success' we've all been sold. I studied hard. I got into a good college. I began investing in the stock market. I built I.I.M.U.N. with one goal: to take it to every last city, and then, every last corner of the world. I wasn't chasing a paycheck; I was chasing a legacy that meant something.

My earnings were such that I remember turning twenty-five and buying myself a Mercedes. It felt cool. Sharp. Like I'd arrived. But within days, I found myself asking: *What next?* A Porsche? A private jet? A personal island?

I looked around and realized, not one of my friends had done the same. By the world's standards, I was ahead. But instead of feeling proud, I felt… empty.

Somewhere along the way, that chase started to feel… off.

I couldn't see where it stopped. Or what I was even driving toward. Surprisingly, after the initial few days, I barely drove the car at all. Then something deeply personal happened. The kind of thing that shakes your frame but strengthens your foundation. It made me pause and ask, for real:

So, what exactly am I chasing?

I still remember the feeling. Externally, things were going well. I.I.M.U.N. was growing.

But inside, a quiet discomfort had begun to stir. Was I doing it to make a difference?

Or to prove I could? Was I building to contribute? Or building so I wouldn't feel left behind? Society calls it a midlife crisis… haha.

That's when I realized. I hadn't been growing roots. I'd just been collecting milestones. Soon, I turned I.I.M.U.N. into a full-fledged NGO. I stopped trying to 'come first' in visibility, growth, or reach. I stopped looking sideways. I started listening inward.

I chose to take no salary. Even the proceeds of this book go to I.I.M.U.N., not as charity... but as clarity.

I was fortunate. I had investments that gave me stability. And yes, my family supports me. I don't take that lightly. But that allowed me to make a different kind of decision. I live alongside my parents, but alone. I don't measure I.I.M.U.N.'s success in terms of the number of conferences or engagements anymore. I measure it in impact, in the eyes that light up, the ideas that sparked, the one student who said, 'This changed something for me.' I don't feel the need to travel to all events, nor speak much. In fact, I barely travel at all. I prefer the youth to lead the youth. Now I:

- Help young people from the I.I.M.U.N. network, across fields, across cities;
- Create without the pressure to perform;
- Say 'no' to things that look impressive but feel hollow.

And yes, people think this is impractical.

'You're wasting your potential.'

'You could build something massive.'

'This won't last forever.'

They might be right. But here's the thing. I'm not trying to build something that lasts forever. I'm trying to live something that feels right, as of now. This isn't a retirement speech. I still work hard. I still have dreams. But the way I define growth has changed.

It's not about more meetings. It's about more meaning.

Not about growing a following. But growing up myself.

What have I learnt?

You don't have to give up ambition. You just have to make sure your ambition doesn't consume *you*. By now, you've seen the picture.

Hustle isn't evil. Money isn't evil. Ambition isn't evil.

You may never open a bank account at all. Here's the account you actually live with:

What am I earning?	*What am I losing?*
Skills	Sleep
Praise	Peace
Attention	Intention
Opportunities	Time with people I love
Influence	Influence over myself

No audit will catch it. No chart will show it. But your soul knows the numbers, and the balance sheet of life doesn't lie.

You don't have to quit your job, meditate in the mountains, give up your phone, or become a monk with a podcast. You just have to pause long enough to ask: Is this working for me? Or just working me into the ground?

And if the answer makes you uncomfortable, that's not failure. That's feedback.

You'll be told, 'Don't settle.' But no one tells you what not to settle for.

Maybe don't settle for:

- Noise disguised as relevance;
- Speed disguised as progress;
- Followers disguised as friends;
- Riches disguised as respect.

Settle only for what lets you sleep peacefully and wake up honestly. There's no one-size-fits-all formula. These are a few questions that helped me:

- What do I want?
- Why do I want it?

- Does it have any real value, or is it an impulse?
- Am I okay to pay the physical or mental cost?

If your answer changes over time, that's okay. That's growth. That's the real return on investment. Maybe life isn't about finding 'balance' once. Maybe it's about building your own balance sheet, with awareness, alignment, and the courage to revise it when needed.

And that, my friends, is my understanding of hustle, happiness, and the holy rupee.

Building the Country, Not Just Unicorns

11.

'Business is not just about profit. It is about purpose. And sometimes, that purpose is freedom.'

Yes, actual freedom.

Let's rewind to a lesser-known truth about India's freedom struggle. It wasn't just fought on the streets. Or debated in Constituent Assembly halls. It was also quietly bankrolled by India's business class.

From Jamnalal Bajaj, the industrialist who Gandhi called his 'fifth son,' to GD Birla, who provided the Mahatma shelter, printing presses, and travel funds, India's fight for independence was supported not just with slogans, but with cheques.

These weren't businessmen looking for government contracts; they were patriots funding a revolution. Many of India's biggest business houses today, Bajaj, Birla, Godrej, and even Tata, were part of this larger vision, that business must serve the nation.

So, when we talk about building a Viksit Bharat today, a prosperous, self-reliant, and future-ready India by 2047, we must remember that industry has always been a pillar of nation-building.

And now, it must rise again. Not just to create wealth. But to create impact.

Like after Independence, the government laid down the laws, and Indian industry quietly laid down the infrastructure.

- The Tatas built Air India when aviation was still a luxury for royals. They didn't wait for policy; they created possibility.

- Godrej designed India's first ballot boxes; literally building the hardware of our democracy.
- Infosys and Wipro made India a software superpower when the West still saw us as a land of snake charmers.
- Reliance created retail, telecom, and digital ecosystems that today power everything from UPI to your shows on Jio Hotstar.
- Aditya Birla Group made the hard infrastructure through companies in cement and aluminium. And then diversified to lifestyle, where they have taken over foreign brands like Allen Solly and Van Heusen.
- More recently, during COVID-19, Serum Institute delivered vaccines not just to India, but also to the world.

These weren't passion projects. They were purposeful profits. The point?

India didn't rise because of foreign capital or colonial charity. It rose because its businesses bet on its people. Now, in 2025, as we stand on the edge of history, just 22 years from 2047, we must ask:

Will today's businesses help build a Viksit Bharat, or will they just build unicorns that are focused on making the founders Viksit? Because this time, the war isn't for independence. It's for economic sovereignty. We can't fight it with loss-making companies and Shark Tank scripts. We need founders who think like freedom fighters, not just fundraisers.

While as of August 2025, India boasts of 119 unicorns, let's examine some of these companies:

- Bigbasket: The place where India shops its groceries from is yet bleeding losses quarter after quarter and is propped up only by endless cash infusions.

- Ola: Touted as India's answer to Uber, has its mobility arm continuing to bleed capital even as the company chases acquisitions.
- Paytm: Pioneering India's digital-payments revolution, the platform is still struggling to turn a profit on core financial services.
- OYO: A hospitality disruptor with a global footprint, OYO is yet perennially dependent on debt and equity raises to stay afloat.

These names dominate headlines, but only twenty-nine of these unicorns are profitable. Let's be real: They're still struggling to stand on their own feet, forget carrying a nation on their shoulders.

In a country where farmers still die by suicide, where millions remain unemployed, and where basic amenities are a daily struggle, how long can we celebrate businesses that survive on life support?

The truth is stark. You can't build a nation on broken balance sheets. Because if it is, it's not a business of tomorrow. It's just another bubble.

They themselves can 'Flip their Cart' anytime.

Here's the harsh reality for all carts that have flipped. We are not just exporting equity, we are exporting losses. We are sending billions abroad in hope and hype, and what we're getting in return are layoffs, PR apologies, and empty chairs. We are short-selling the India story ourselves!

These companies may have Indian names. Indian founders. Indian users. But peel back the glossy branding, and you'll find something quietly dangerous underneath. Ownership that no longer lives here.

They say the British came for spices and stayed for 200 years. Today, investors come for your app and stay for your stake.

When discussing colonization, we usually imagine red coats, East India ships, and the stolen Kohinoor. But make no mistake, colonization has not ended. It has now got a different form.

In 2025, it doesn't come with gunpowder. It comes with equity contracts. The battlefield isn't your land… It's your data, your equity, and your IP.

So, the bigger question is? Are they even founded in India?

Of all unicorns founded by Indians, 109 of them are registered outside of India!

Even more dangerous is: Are they *owned* by the Indians who founded them?

- Flipkart

  Founded by two Indian engineers, Flipkart was once the poster child of Indian e-commerce. Today? 81% of it is owned by Walmart, headquartered in Arkansas, USA. That means every time you 'shop local' on Flipkart, most profits cross the ocean.
- Paytm (One97 Communications)

  Hailed as a fintech pioneer and vocal flag-bearer of 'Made in India'. Look beneath the PR, and you'll find that as of Q3 FY25, 56.2% of its shares are held by Foreign Institutional Investors (FIIs), including Alibaba's Ant Group, a Chinese company, which at one point held over 25% alone.

  Swadeshi slogans. *Videshi* stakes.
- Urban Company

  As of September 2025, the company that we use to fix everything at home has 68.15% owned by Foreign Institutional Investors.

- Swiggy
  Prosus (formerly Naspers), a Dutch company, owns 25%. When you add the stakes of other international players like Accel and Tencent-linked entities, foreign control surpasses the halfway mark in boardroom influence, even if not always in pure shareholding.

Because when your cap table is 80% foreign and your profits get siphoned off to some Cayman Island trust fund, are you really 'building Bharat'?

No cap, bro, you're just a white-collar vendor with an Indian logo!

Let's put it bluntly: if your startup hits a billion-dollar valuation but your decision-making sits in Silicon Valley, who wins? India? Or the fund manager who's never stepped foot in Bharat, but now decides your startup's future?

This isn't business. This is digital colonization in beta mode. If we're not careful, we'll end up with a digital economy that looks Indian on the outside, but is hollow on the inside.

So, what's the solution?

No, the answer isn't to stop all foreign investment. India needs capital. Global partnerships. Strategic alliances. But we must also ask for balance. Because ownership matters. Not just on paper, but in spirit. We fought for political independence in 1947. In 2025, the fight is for digital and economic independence. Not with slogans, but with patents and boardroom seats.

Because in the long run, it's not enough to say 'Made in India' if the money ends up 'Parked in Singapore'.

So, what does it look like to build *truly Indian*? To stay local, not just in logo, but in leadership, loyalty, and legacy?

Let's begin with a name you definitely know: Byju's.

Launched in 2011 with the dream to transform education, Byju's became one of the most valuable edtech startups. It raised billions, ran ads during the FIFA World Cup, even hired Messi to be the face, sponsored cricket teams, and became a global symbol of 'India's startup story'.

But what began as a massive PR campaign ended as a very messy and cautionary tale:

- Mounting losses.
- Layoffs in the thousands.
- Disillusioned investors and legal cases.
- Broken trust with students, teachers, and parents.
- Hundreds of lawsuits.

The founders made millions, while millions suffered. Now, the funny part is this: we travel to cities, small and big, but wherever we went and spoke to students and management in schools, the troubling statistic was that not even 5% used their services.

Brand recall was great, but not the company itself. This did not deter the company, which was constantly raising Series A, B, and C. I think they would have raised more rounds than the alphabet would allow. Slowly, every young entrepreneur wanted to be the next Bjyu's.

But no one was seeing what was happening on the inside. No customers = a hollow story.

When the truth started coming out, it wasn't just a failed company. People crunched the real numbers. It became the poster child of what happens when hype outruns humility.

Because…

Hype is not heritage.

Funding is not the foundation.

And valuation is not value.

Now contrast that with a few organizations you may not see trending on Twitter, which have quietly changed lives, communities, and policy, without chasing the unicorn badge.

1. Pratham
Started in the slums of Mumbai, Pratham grew into one of the largest education NGOs in the country. Their Annual Status of Education Report (ASER) is cited by the Government of India, economists, and global education experts. They've taught millions of children to read, write, and do math, not in air-conditioned studios, but in under-resourced villages and urban shadows.

2. Goonj
They didn't build a startup; they redefined dignity. By turning urban waste into a rural resource, Goonj helped during floods, droughts, and cyclones, all while maintaining zero marketing gimmicks. Their campaign, 'Not Just a Piece of Cloth,' destigmatized menstruation across many villages in rural India.

3. Amul
Started in 1946 by farmers in Gujarat, Amul is perhaps India's most remarkable business success story, *without ever being called a startup*. Born out of a cooperative movement, it empowered millions of dairy farmers and created a ₹50,000 plus crore brand that's still owned by the people. Not a founder. A collective. It's not a valuation story. But a value revolution.

4. I.I.M.U.N.
Founded in the same year as Byju's, 2011, I.I.M.U.N. didn't sell subscriptions or push premium plans. It built something more

challenging to price: awareness, dialogue, and citizenship. Today, over one lakh schools across India have hosted or participated in Model UN-style engagements; all but nineteen schools that started before us can trace their origin to I.I.M.U.N.'s quiet influence in one way or another. No commercialization. Students are empowering others via leadership and social impact activities to think, speak, and lead with an Indian lens. The result? A new breed of lawyers, doctors, civil servants, and politicians is spreading their own versions of India.

After all, you can raise ₹1,000 crores. But what good is it if you collapse under your own ambition? You can trend. But if your users feel betrayed, your brand is bankrupt.

Because India doesn't need 10,000 pitch decks, it needs 100 institutions that stay for 100 years. Like Reliance. Like HDFC. Like Bajaj.

Talking about Bajaj, it was best summarized by Late Madhur Bajaj, who was on our foundation's Advisory Board, 'Don't just build to be known. Build to be missed.'

Combine that with what Piyush Goyal, India's Commerce Minister in 2025, said, 'We don't need more companies that only make food delivery convenient for the rich.'

You have got a roadmap. Well, I think there's space for food delivery as well. But let's also create meaningful businesses. Not just platforms to binge-watch or allow us to binge-eat.

If your company shuts down tomorrow, will anyone outside your funding circle care?

That is the test. Not valuation. Contribution.

Because if your name disappears from TechCrunch but stays in the hearts of students, farmers, or forgotten communities …

then congratulations. You've already created more value than most unicorns ever will.

Another important aspect is that we rush young people into creation. We are obsessed with young CEOs, Forbes thirty Under 30, and overnight IPOs, but we forget:

Some of the strongest businesses weren't built by prodigies. *There's no such thing as a late bloomer. Just deep rooters.*

So let's kill the myth right now. You don't need to build the next big thing by 25. Or 35. Or even 55. They were built by people who had lived, failed, worked odd jobs, and *then* built empires. Take Colonel Sanders, yes, the white-haired, suit-wearing mascot behind KFC.

Do you know when he built the empire? Age 65. After failing as a lawyer, losing a gas station, and being rejected over a thousand times with his chicken recipe. He didn't pivot. He persisted. In the end, he didn't just fry chicken. He fried every ageist stereotype in business.

Take Ray Kroc, the man who turned McDonald's into a global phenomenon. He joined the brothers *after* they had a restaurant at age 52, after selling milkshake machines door-to-door.

His genius idea? Simple. Systems. Discipline. Scale. He wasn't chasing cool. He was chasing consistency.

Even in India, some of the most iconic business leaders started later than you think:

- Dhirubhai Ambani built Reliance from a small cloth trading business in his mid-30s, but the empire didn't take off overnight. It scaled post his 50s through relentless reinvention, street-smart strategy, and bold risk-taking that built one of India's biggest conglomerates.
- Narayana Murthy started Infosys at 38 after quitting his job and borrowing ₹10,000 from his wife. It wasn't flashy, it

wasn't fast, but it was foundational. Today, Infosys is a global IT force and a blueprint for ethical entrepreneurship.

These weren't kids with dorm room dreams. These were thinkers, planners, late-bloomers, and builders. We live in an age where:

- 22-year-olds feel 'too old' to start something new.
- People panic if they aren't viral by their third post.
- Founders fear FOMO more than flawed business models.

Here's the reminder: You're not behind. You're *becoming*. Take your time. Learn. Unlearn. Intern. Fail. Work under someone smarter than you or having better skillsets than you. Build slowly.

Fall in love with systems, not just scale.

Fall in love with boredom, because that's where breakthroughs are born.

Maybe your business will:

- Serve five villages, not 5 million people.
- Hire ten loyal people, not 1,000 LinkedIn followers.
- Make ₹5 crores a year, not ₹500 crores in funding.

And that's still valid. Still powerful. Still yours.

So, whether you're 16 or 61… You haven't missed your moment. You're just marinating. And we all know, the longer the marination, the stronger the flavour.

So far, we've spoken about building slowly. Building ethically. Building for the long game. But now, let's go a step further.

Because it's not just about building for yourself. Or even for your company. It's about building for Bharat.

Today's India doesn't just need more unicorns. It needs conscious capitalists, people who solve, not just scale. People who realize that profit isn't the opposite of purpose, it's just a tool to fund it.

Because a good business doesn't just sell, it uplifts. It listens. It educates. It solves real problems, without waiting for a government scheme or CSR mandate.

We're a country that solved water scarcity with step-wells. That managed waste through zero-waste temples. That used cow dung for insulation, neem for pesticides, and built sustainable systems long before 'sustainability' became a Silicon Valley pitch deck. Now imagine if Indian businesses embraced this wisdom. Imagine if we created startups not just for users, but for *upaya (purposeful means)*.

A good 21st-century home-grown example is:

Zoho, a global SaaS success story, runs its headquarters out of rural Tamil Nadu, hires local talent, and quietly proves that you don't need to shift to the West to win globally. The founder also lives a quiet, low-key life. This isn't just business. This is modern seva.

Another one which I have closely observed is the Piramal Group, whose entire identity is built on Seva Bhav. A large amount of their profits are ploughed into making their local communities better. And it's not publicized, it's not put on billboards or campaigns. Their Piramal Foundation has 'Karuna Fellowship' where girls from marginalized sections of our society are trained and given opportunities to contribute on existing projects. Then, they are placed or equipped to start ecosystems on their own.

This is a real impact. There's an old Indian idea, *'Artha should serve dharma.'*

In other words, wealth should serve the right values. That doesn't mean you can't be ambitious. Or that you must give everything away.

But ask yourself:

- Is your product helping people live better?
- Is your team being treated with dignity?
- Are your profits being used to buy something bigger than a new car?

Because you don't need to be a non-profit to be non-toxic.

What ISRO is to space, and what Ayurveda is to health, Indian businesses can be to ethical innovation.

But only if we build with:

- *Viveka* (discernment);
- *Vairagya* (freedom from excess);
- And a deep alignment with India's needs.

If money becomes the goal, you'll always feel poor. But if money becomes the means to solve, to serve, to scale good, you'll never run out of purpose.

'In the 20th century, freedom fighters built the nation.

In the 21st century, it's time for founders to do the same.'

50 Shades of Grey

12.

After eleven chapters of decoding everything from love and likes to god and grief, we've reached the chapter that isn't just about the world, but the compass you'll carry through it. We've discussed mental health, gender, money, hustle, heartbreak, and hashtags.

But this... this is about meaning. Not the kind of meaning you find in a textbook or tattoo. The kind you discover quietly, the kind that helps you answer questions like:

- Is it okay to love the same gender?
- Is it okay not to believe in religion?
- Is it okay to be in a relationship while benching someone else?
- If honesty is a value, is bribing your way to a contract wrong, or just realistic?
- Is it ethical to use AI to write your assignment?
- Is it okay to build a billion-dollar business that wipes out thousands of jobs?
- Is it moral to ghost people, parents or partner to protect your peace?

You've probably asked yourself at least one of these. And if not, you will. Because this is the age of grey zones. In school, we are told:

- Stealing is bad.
- Lying is wrong.
- Respect your elders.
- Study hard and succeed.

But what if your elders are abusive? What if success isn't what society defines for you? What if the truth sounds like fake news?

That's where morality, values, and ethics come in, not as rules, but as reflections. Let's be honest, no generation has faced more moral dilemmas in more places at once than yours.

You're being asked to:

- Pick a definitive career path;
- Save the planet;
- Fight for social justice;
- Stay fit;
- Voice yourself but respectfully;
- Be kind;
- Be real while figuring out what you believe in and what you don't.

So here's my offer: Just like every chapter,

I won't tell you what's right. I will share what I've learnt by getting it wrong. And in the process, perhaps it will help you ask better questions.

Because sometimes morality isn't a line. It's a lens.

And this chapter, like the rest of this book, is an invitation to build a moral compass that doesn't point north, but inward.

Because in a world divided between cancel culture and complete chaos, your inner court will matter more than outer validation. Before you decide what's moral for you, maybe it helps to ask, *Where did these ideas even come from?*

Morality wasn't handed down from the sky on an iCloud drive. It was created. Interpreted. Reinvented. Sometimes by kings. Sometimes by prophets. Sometimes by philosophers who stared too long into the abyss.

In the West, morality began with commandments, quite literally. Whether it was the Ten Commandments, the teachings of the Church, or the strict codes of Puritan society, morality was seen as a list of divine dos and don'ts.

Apparently, what is written in books that we have already covered has changed with the times. :D

But break them? You're a sinner. Obey them? You're a saint.

It was simple. But also… not.

This model left no room for grey. Only guilt.

Then came the philosophers: Aristotle believed in 'virtue ethics', the idea that being moral isn't about following rules but becoming a good person through habit and balance.

Immanuel Kant took the opposite route. He believed morality comes from duty. That certain things are always wrong, no matter the outcome. Lying, for instance, is wrong, even if it saves a life.

Jean-Paul Sartre, one of my other favourite rebels, didn't believe morality was handed down from heaven; he thought you built it.

'Man is nothing else but what he makes of himself.'

To Sartre, morality wasn't a divine rulebook. It was a choice. A burden. A freedom.

In a world without inherent meaning, *you* create the meaning. But here's the catch: You don't get to blame others, whether it is god, society, or your upbringing.

And that, in a nutshell, is how Western morality evolved:

From divine rules to philosophical frameworks to existential chaos.

However, the Indian concept of morality wasn't built on commandments. It was built on context. We called it Dharma.

In the *Bhagavad Gita*, Arjuna is told not to run from war, but to fight because it's his duty.

Chanakya didn't preach honesty at all costs. He preached statecraft, even if it meant deception for the greater good.

In the Upanishads, you won't find a list of sins; you'll find questions. Questions about the self. About truth. About the illusion of right and wrong.

Even the 'gods' or superhumans, as I would like to call them, weren't morally perfect. Krishna bent the rules. Shiva broke them. Rama exiled his wife for public perception, a move that still sparks ethical debates.

Morality, in Indian philosophy, wasn't a checkbox. Maybe that's why Indian culture has always had room for contradiction: A renunciate who lives with no possessions and a king who builds golden temples… both are respected.

A warrior who fights and a sage who forgives, both doing their dharma.

Therefore, morality isn't universal. It's cultural, contextual, and evolving.

But here's the twist: Just because morality is flexible doesn't mean it's meaningless.

Before you start justifying any action, and sing Frank Sinatra's, *My Way...*

Please note: It means you have to think. To choose. To build a compass that isn't borrowed, but earned. That's why this chapter isn't about handing you answers. It's about giving you the tools to ask the right questions.

Let me share with you what I consider moral or immoral. But considering we've spoken only the truth, let me confess: It's not a rule book, it's a mirror. Not every situation has a binary answer.

But over time, I've started recognizing a few patterns, a kind of moral math that helps me navigate the noise.

What is immoral to me?

- Deliberate harm, physical, emotional, psychological, especially when disguised as 'help'.
- Exploitation of people, emotions, resources, and power.
- Deception, especially when the truth could heal or protect.
- Decorative virtue, which is saying the right thing when you're doing the wrong thing, just to look good.

What's unethical for me?

- Profiting from someone else's ignorance or helplessness.
- Taking credit for someone else's work (or AI's) as your own with zero thought or learning.
- Staying silent in the face of injustice, not because you're scared, but because it's 'not your problem'.
- Convenient morality… being principled when it's easy and silent when it's not.

But here's the honest bit, life isn't this clear. There's a massive middle ground. That shadowy zone is called grey. And that's where real dilemmas live.

Let me give you a couple of them to ponder over. Steve Jobs: Visionary. But reportedly yelled at and overworked employees in the name of excellence.

Is it okay to berate someone if you are pushing them towards excellence?

Greta Thunberg: A teenager who skipped school to speak to the world.

Is breaking the rules moral, and then is it okay to say that you are fighting for a higher cause?

Zepto and 10-minute delivery: Feels magical when you're

hungry. But what about the rider weaving through traffic at 10 p.m. in the rain?

Is efficiency worth the ethical toll?

Or the closest one for some:

If a person cheats in a relationship but later comes clean, begs for forgiveness, and transforms, is that unforgivable? These aren't 'yes or no' questions. They're 'how,' 'why,' and 'what now?' questions.

Your answers to them will define your morality more than any quote, law, or Instagram reel ever could. For me, morality isn't just what you do. It's why you did it, and who you became after.

But if morality is about what we do and why we do it, values are the anchors that hold us steady when everything else is in flux. They're not just words on vision boards. They're the invisible forces behind your everyday choices, from how you treat a waiter to how you respond to betrayal.

After meeting all kinds of people from different walks of life and messing up more times than I can count, here are the things that help me remain the main character of my story:

1. No Cap

I know, lies are easier. They look better. They help you avoid uncomfortable situations. I have lied on multiple occasions, out of fear or to protect someone. One such instance was when I lied for the first time in a relationship, when I was in college and told my then-girl friend that I was not friends with the ex. She did not want me to even talk to her. I assured myself I was not doing anything wrong, but turns out the girlfriend did not think so. All I can say is it was a tough few weeks. Years later, I realized it was never worth it. Not just to others, but to myself.

Truth isn't always pretty. It may lead to challenging circumstances, but it's always grounding. So, speak the truth.

No cap, I also believe in what French Philosopher, Voltaire said, 'Everything you say should be true, but not everything true should be said.'

2. Heart Over Hype

In a world where everyone is promoting self-care, there is much more than you. Not out of pity. Not saviour syndrome. Just the ability to understand someone's mess, without judging it.

Now I have been a very judgemental human being; I used to judge everyone and everything till about Grade 8 for sure. I shared a deeply personal experience with my closest friend in school, and he went and mentioned it to everyone. It was about my mum and dad; I did not want everyone talking about it. I felt bad, and since then I have learnt never to judge anyone and definitely not to use such information. Choose heart over hype.

But sometimes, compassion means setting boundaries, and yes, you can be kind and clear at the same time.

3. No Beta Energy

Some of these thoughts I have written about have been long-held truths that I was worried I shouldn't share because they might offend people. This book could have been written three years ago as well. But courage is important. The courage to: Speak. Act. Stand alone, especially when it's uncool to do so.

Another incident is when I was told not to act against corrupt practices in schools. This is when we organized our first conference. It was common to give an 'Admin fee' to the school. All vendors should. But I.I.M.U.N. is a youth-run non-profit; we refused to cave in and did a sting operation on one school that asked for a bribe. I was 19, the year was 2011, and to date, we have never given bribes, nor do I advocate it. The school boycotted us for 12 years, but has now recently come around.

Keep no beta energy. The kind that doesn't get you claps, just clarity. And it is in that effort that I pen this book.

4. Staying Low-key

Growing up as a teenager, I was quick to get offended, and I still sometimes do. Ego is truly EGO: Everlasting Gory Overconfidence. Emphasis on everlasting. Because no matter how many books I write, posts I make, or panels I sit on, I now know I can still be wrong. And I need to be okay with that. We are but a speck in the universe, which we comprehend.

Now, I did not think like this all along. I was a presumptuous teenager who most of the time thought no end of himself. After all, I strived to be the smartest one in the room. Then one day, I met Shashi Tharoor. End of story.

So, stay low-key.

5. On the Grind

Not as punishment. But as devotion to growth. Whether it's meditating, showing up on time (I am yet grappling with this one), or doing the hard thing first. I was travelling to Japan in 2017 for an I.I.M.U.N. Conference, the train or shinkansen was going to get late by 30 seconds. All of us on the train got a note saying 'Sorry for the delay'. I yet miraculously managed to reach my meeting 15 minutes late, but missed the meeting. You want to learn discipline, take a flight to Tokyo.

The problem is I am yet to fully imbibe this, as my most recent happenstance shows. While travelling to the UK, I got late to visit 10 Downing Street, and therefore was politely told by the person I was meeting that it would be futile to have a discussion at that point. Requested a meeting again, but now the brown man has been replaced by a white one.

Being on the grind isn't glamorous. But it's sacred.

6. What's for Dinner Tonight

The one skill we all have, but sometimes gets extinguished by society. This is the reason this book exists. This is the reason I ask annoying questions. And this is the reason I'll probably rewrite my definition of morality five years from now.

For me, this was inbuilt. I absolutely loved asking questions. I remember finishing my assignments in school and then going to the next one and raising questions to my teacher, much to the dismay of the remaining students. The questions have kept changing, but I keep questioning nonetheless.

What's for dinner tonight? Keeps me evolving. Keeps me alive. Keeps me hungry.

7. No one's Watching, but You are

When your words, actions, and thoughts align, even when no one's watching. It's easy to have integrity in public. Harder in private. But that's the real test. This happened when I was given the opportunity to cheat in a chess game when I was ten. An elderly gentleman told me, go to the bathroom, and we will help you with clues of what you should play next. The tournament was the U-16 championships in Abu Dhabi. I could have easily fallen prey, but what is victory if it is stolen and not earned? Plus, to be honest, fear kept my integrity. Is fear the best place for integrity to arise? No. But whatever helps you start.

Just as importantly, here are the values I've learnt to unlearn and some of which are work in progress:

- Hustle: It'll just leave you bustling. We had an entire chapter on this.
- Blind obedience: Just because something is traditional doesn't make it right. I used to follow this in case of religion. You know what happened thereafter.
- Fake kindness: Niceness without a backbone. Words without action. I have a tendency to say things which please people. I hate to disappoint. So, I'm working on this.
- Moral superiority: Believing you're better just because you're 'more intelligent' or aware. No longer there, if you just read enough of the right books, you will realize the importance of dissolving the I.

My values have evolved. What I thought were good values at sixteen changed at twenty-six. And that's okay, as long as you're evolving, too. Because the goal isn't to collect aura points. The goal is to live a life that feels aligned.

So here we are! Not at the end of the book. But like in all other chapters, at the beginning of your inquiry with truth. You will see your friends' posts, which will be filtered lives, and wonder if you're falling behind. You will feel the need to be validated; I still do, at times.

You will be tempted to cheat in the exam, once, just this once. You will see people being applauded for hollow things.

And you may get punished for doing what's right. So, who decides the rules?

Another favourite French philosopher Albert Camus once said, *'Integrity has no need of rules.'*

But I believe you will need to build your own. In a world full of colours, the human eye can only see red, green, blue and many of their combinations.

One thing that has helped me build my colour palette was, 'Will I be okay living with this choice?'

You've read stories, theories, questions, and contradictions.

Now it's your turn.

To define your morality.

To choose your values.

To build your own shades of grey.

That's the point, isn't it? Stay Young, Wired and (not) Woke.

If you have an opinion about the chapter or the book, please do share it with me. I would love to hear from you. :D And even if you don't, I'd be happiest to hear from you.

Afterword

Dearest Gentle Reader,

Before you go, this, to my mind, is the biggest question of them all.

So, what does it mean to be Indian… today?

Is it in the syllables of your name?

Or the verve with which you sing the national anthem before a movie?

Is it in the food on your plate, or the fire in your debates?

Is it touching your parents' feet, or questioning what they believe?

Is it fasting during Navratri, or feasting on Netflix on Diwali eve?

Is it being a Bhakt or someone who loves the opposition?

Why are we forced to pick in every situation?

This book has wandered through twelve terrains of minds and mantras, of rupees and rains. From mental health to moral roads, from heartbreak reels to startup codes.

We spoke of gender beyond binaries and buzz, and love, not the filmy kind, but the one that does.

We questioned fame, influence, digital highs, and found meaning where the algorithm dies.

We walked through faith, stripped of fear, and saw god as he is, my dear.

We decoded AI's thinking spree, and asked if purpose will ever be glitch-free.

We stood at the crossroads of cash and calm, of Dharma, deadlines, and inner alarm.

We spoke of ethics, messy and grey, where choices matter more than what you say.

And through it all, one thread was spun. A quiet voice whispered, 'You're still the one.'

The one whose ancestors watched the stars, who carried epics in memory, not memoirs.

You're the one who can build and bend, with Google tabs and a guru's lens. You're the spark in a billion dreams, the rhythm in this nation's memes.

Some days, you'll feel certain. Other days, unsure.

Some choices will echo your lineage. Some may ask for a detour.

And that's okay. Because identity isn't an answer, it's a becoming.

Maybe being Indian is not in the rituals you perform, but in the questions you carry.

Not in how loudly you declare it, but how quietly it shapes your view.

It's in the pauses you take. In the metaphors you make. In the mangoes you miss in May (yes, I love mangoes). In the kindness that stays when the world walks away.

You may speak ten languages. Live in cities with snow or a skyline. Hold a passport from India or not, and that's still fine.

But your imagination, your instinct, your insight will always echo a civilisation that once mapped the stars, and now maps the soul.

You are not just from India.

You are a continuation of it.

A living thread in its evolving song.

And perhaps the most Indian thing you'll ever do is to reflect deeply before you define what that means for you.

Jai Hind!